OPENIN
DOOR!
to
QUALITY
WRITING

Ideas for writing
inspired by great writers
for ages 10 to 13

BOB COX

Crown House Publishing Limited
www.crownhouse.co.uk

First published by

Crown House Publishing Ltd
Crown Buildings, Bancyfelin, Carmarthen, Wales, SA33 5ND, UK
www.crownhouse.co.uk

and

Crown House Publishing Company LLC
PO Box 2223, Williston, VT 05495
www.crownhousepublishing.com

First published 2016.

Extracts from *The Castle* and *Metamorphosis* by Franz Kafka are reproduced with kind permission of Wordsworth Classics.
'The Magnifying Glass' by Walter de la Mare is reproduced with kind permission of The Literary Trustees of Walter de la
Mare and The Society of Authors as their representative.
'A Garden at Night' © James Reeves from *Complete Poems for Children* (Faber Finds).
Reprinted by permission of the James Reeves Estate.

British Library Cataloguing-in-Publication Data
A catalogue entry for this book is available
from the British Library.

Print ISBN 978-178583014-3
Mobi ISBN 978-178583125-6
ePub ISBN 978-178583126-3
ePDF ISBN 978-178583127-0

LCCN 2015959143

Printed and bound in the UK by
Gomer Press, Llandysul, Ceredigion

For Becky, with love

Contents

Acknowledgements

I have been able to develop 'Opening Doors' into a series of books thanks to the feedback and encouragement from schools across the UK, and their trialling of materials. It is much appreciated and, indeed, inspiring to hear from so many schools using the ideas.

In particular, I would like to thank staff and pupils from:

St Augustine's Catholic Primary School, Frimley, Surrey

Balcarras School and associated teaching alliance schools, Cheltenham, Gloucestershire

Boxgrove Primary School and teaching alliance schools, Guildford, Surrey

Broadstone First School, Poole, Dorset

Church Crookham Junior School, Fleet, Hampshire

Churchfields Junior School, South Woodford, Redbridge

Crofton Hammond Infants School, Hampshire

Epsom Partnership in Surrey

Fort Hill Community School, Basingstoke, Hampshire

Frogmore Junior School, Hampshire

Furze Platt Infants School, Maidenhead, RBWM

Furze Platt Secondary School, Maidenhead, RBWM

Hawley Primary School, Hampshire

Hook Junior School, Hampshire

Netley Abbey Primary School, Hampshire

Portsmouth Grammar School, Hampshire

Ravenscote Junior School, Camberley, Surrey

Ringwood National Teaching School, Hampshire

Robin Hood Junior School, Sutton, Surrey

Roch Community Primary School, Pembrokeshire

Saturday Challenge Enrichment Centre, Fleet, Hampshire

St Francis RC Primary School, Maidenhead, RBWM

St Teresa's Catholic Primary School, Wokingham, Berkshire

The Grange Community Junior School, Farnborough, Hampshire

Wandsworth Local Authority

Westfields Junior School, Yateley, Hampshire

Wicor Primary School, Fareham, Hampshire

Teachers and schools in Poole and across Dorset, Surrey and Wandsworth

Also:

Potential Plus UK

Osiris Educational

And especially:

Crown House Publishing for their continued amazing support and enthusiasm.

although [the Brontës] don't write many novels ... they've tried lots of different genres, they've experimented. It's been like a literary kind of workshop – the four of them working together and so by the time they're writing *Wuthering Heights* or *Jane Eyre*, they're very sophisticated users of those forces.

John Bowen and Ann Dinsdale, 'The Brontës'
Early Writings: Combining Fantasy and Fact'

Introduction

Opening Doors to Quality Writing is a companion book to *Opening Doors to Famous Poetry and Prose* (2014). There are two books, one for ages 10 to 13 and one for ages 6 to 9. The idea is that teachers will be supported, in flexible and creative ways, to use quality literary texts to stimulate quality writing. My theme has continued to be the exploration of poetry and prose from long ago, sometimes termed 'literary heritage' texts. My aim is to suggest ways in which the evident quality of the writing can be exploited by schools to develop exciting journeys in reading, writing, speaking and listening for their pupils. I am seeing many teachers successfully using the scope and depth which literature can offer to inspire high standards, mastery learning and, above all, a love of language in its many forms. My criteria for choosing the texts has been that they support the need for greater knowledge of literature from the past and provide the scope needed for deeper learning in English

All the units should help you to make links from understanding the challenging texts to maximising the huge potential for quality writing. I hope your pupils will enjoy the writing ideas suggested and that you and your pupils will be inspired to devise your own! You should find the level of expectation goes up and, with it, the children's writing should become more quirky, creative and unusual – after all, it's great writers who have inspired the class! In this book, I have been able to include examples of remarkable pupils' work, of all abilities, and have included a story of my own. I am always encouraging teachers to write with their pupils, so it's a way of showing that it can be a natural thing to do. Writing creatively maintains my own awareness of how difficult and enjoyable it can be and, since we are encouraging quality writing, we can all be partners in the process.

In my extensive travels as a teacher and an educational consultant, I have often found that progress is limited either by a model which becomes too much of a straightjacket or by an unwillingness to adapt the model to suit particular classes or pupils. Feedback from *Opening Doors to Famous Poetry and Prose* has frequently emphasised the confidence which can develop when ideas are used as a starting point, not an end game – for example:

Thank you for reigniting our love of quality texts and giving us fantastic planning and teaching ideas to encourage all abilities to access the texts.

Churchfields Junior School Conference, 2015

Support and enthusiasm from teachers is essential. It is the teachers who will take ideas deeper, invent new questions and present their lessons in new planning shapes. The books (and the conferences I run) are designed to signpost ways to access a harder curriculum so that confidence and self-evaluation can grow. When challenging texts become the norm in classroom practice, there are significant implications for methodology and resourcing, so the 'Opening Doors' series is a complement to approaches being trialled in schools which involve all learners working on the same content and with the same objectives.

Overwhelmingly, however, teachers have been asking for more of the quality texts themselves and more ways in which all abilities can access them. So, here are fifteen units of work which should help to stimulate many innovative ways for all your pupils to enjoy literature and write with originality. Schools working with the 'Opening Doors' strategies have tended to report:

❦ More teacher empowerment and confidence.

❦ More knowledge building for pupils and teachers.

❦ A growing confidence with literature, including poetry.

❦ A tendency to move to using 'English' as the subject name rather than 'literacy'.

❦ Planning from the top becoming a norm.

❦ Planning for mastery learning becoming a norm.

❦ Improved comprehension skills.

❦ Improved quality writing and associated excitement.

'Opening Doors' is intended to add a more challenging dimension to English teaching, but all learners can find that doors have been opened because access is always emphasised. The diagram on page 4 provides a framework for the many ways in which quality writing can be achieved.

The pattern you will find across the units marks out the major principles which can support a richer diet in English:

❦ Texts with scope for creativity and curiosity.

❦ The need for a range of access strategies.

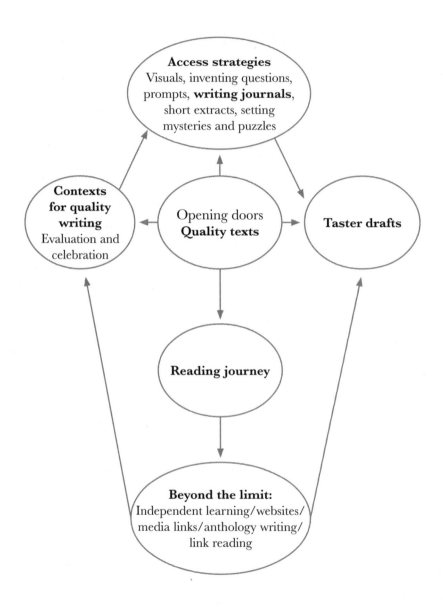

❦ The recommendation to write early on in the process via **taster drafts**.

❦ Using a range of assessment for learning strategies and 'excellent responses' criteria.

❦ Emphasising the wonder of the text revealed.

❦ Offering harder, evaluative questions sooner.

❦ Linking the learning about quality texts with the application required for quality writing.

❦ Including 'beyond the limit' reading and writing ideas at appropriate points.

❦ Planning lessons in shapes which suit the objectives.

Both the diagram and the questions across the units are set out in a radial way with choices, options and routes critical to differentiation methods which can be planned according to progress. At all times, great writers and great writing lead the way so the inspiration comes from them, with pupils guided by the immense talent of their teachers. There is no need to be limited by any single pedagogy. Approaches can be constantly evaluated and altered according to outcomes. I love the feedback I get from teachers telling me they have linked the text with a more modern one, negotiated fresh questions or converted the task into a different medium.

At the heart of the 'Opening Doors' concept is the need for the teachers to use literary texts as starting points for their own invention. That mindset is bound to spread to the pupils. They will be suggesting approaches too – and why not?

Part 1

Opening doors
to prose

Night Encounter

The Woman in White by Wilkie Collins

How well can you introduce a mystery story?

Access strategies

Wilkie Collins is often credited with writing the first mystery story, *The Woman in White* (1859). It's easy to forget that, once upon a time, writing about a mystery was a new concept! The hero of the story, Walter Hartright, is a kind of detective and your pupils will be sampling the style of writing which influenced so many later authors to weave sensational plots around a sleuth. The story was incredibly popular in its own time, and there were even products like perfumes and clothing using the 'Woman in White' branding. Although the novel itself is long, encourage as many of your pupils as possible to try it because it is readable and eventful.

Try using a **key image strategy** to open up access to this famous mystery for all. Which images in this short extract from Chapter 4 stimulate the children's curiosity the most? Why?

[…] in one moment, every drop of blood in my body was brought to a stop by the touch of a hand laid lightly and suddenly on my shoulder from behind me.

I turned on the instant, with my fingers tightening round the handle of my stick.

There, in the middle of the broad, bright high-road – there, as if it had that moment sprung out of the earth or dropped from the heaven – stood the figure of a solitary Woman, dressed from head to foot in white garments, her face bent in grave inquiry on mine, her hand pointing to the dark cloud over London, as I faced her.

Now, use an **explore and explain** learning pathway. The idea is that your pupils are building an understanding of *how* the mystery is set up. They must search for evidence in one group and then move groups to feed back to others. This keeps the pressure on to participate, listen and learn, rather than defer to the most proactive students.

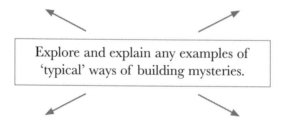

Explore and explain any examples of 'typical' ways of building mysteries.

After switching groups and deepening their learning, ask them to share selected ideas as a whole class and then add your own knowledge. Linking now with the 'beyond the limit' section on page 16 might be useful to incorporate prior learning and **link reading**.

Excellent responses will include:

❦ The first person narrator's fear is shared with us as he experiences it.

❦ Phrases like 'every drop of blood' add detail to the emotional atmosphere and link mental with physical distress. The hands on the stick accentuate this.

❦ The light touch on the shoulder adds to a sense of the unknown. It may not hurt but it prickles the senses.

❦ A one line paragraph makes us read it like a still photograph.

❦ The much longer paragraph, with the dashes marking off an echo of the narrator's astonishment, finally gives us the view we have waited for.

❦ A 'solitary Woman' is perhaps a surprise! Why is there a capital letter for 'Woman'?

❦ The white garments mark out a mystery and they stand out visually. What can white signify?

❦ Why is the hand pointing at the dark cloud?

The questions mount …

Writing a **taster draft** now would exploit the deeper thinking and stimulate original writing. Ask your pupils to use some of the ideas they have learnt from Wilkie Collins in a brief passage. It could introduce a mysterious character in an appropriate setting. No sustained plot is needed at this point, just a taster of the feel of mystery. Drafts should be shared, explored and read out, with more advice given in a **mini-plenary**.

Bob says ...

Do add your own reading experiences at this point. Often we can get so absorbed in spotting techniques that we forget it's the overall power of character creation that endures. Discuss how your pupils feel about the figure in white, whether they have had spooky encounters or felt that sinister sense of the unknown. Which books or poems have the same kind of impact? Does TV or film do it in the same way? The best English lessons find space to explore and explain how we interact with language and how the experience is different for each one of us.

Let's all get inspired by this taster draft by Ethan from Roch Community Primary School:

The crunch of footsteps over rusty leaves fills me with shock, as I jump back into the darkness of the villainous woods, with the trees looking down at me. A young man with an unusual moustache walks past and lights his pipe. Slowly I bend over and walk towards the man; the moonlight showing the way. I tap his shoulder. Trembling with fear I run back before he has a chance to turn around.

Shock fills him. I am gone. The darkness hides me as he, still overpowered with questions, stands shaking like leaves in an autumn wind. Slowly walking back over I tap him again but this time say, 'Is this the way to London?'

Ethan Jones, Year 4

Reading journeys

Now more of the text should be revealed and read out. Expect your pupils to be fascinated as they compare in their minds their taster drafts with this extended piece:

Resource 3

I had now arrived at that particular point of my walk where four roads met – the road to Hampstead, along which I had returned, the road to Finchley, the road to West End, and the road back to London. I had mechanically turned in this latter direction, and was strolling along the lonely high-road – idly wondering, I remember, what the Cumberland young ladies would look like – when, in one moment, every drop of blood in my body was brought to a stop by the touch of a hand laid lightly and suddenly on my shoulder from behind me.

I turned on the instant, with my fingers tightening round the handle of my stick.

There, in the middle of the broad, bright high-road – there, as if it had that moment sprung out of the earth or dropped from the heaven – stood the figure of a solitary Woman, dressed from head to foot in white garments, her face bent in grave inquiry on mine, her hand pointing to the dark cloud over London, as I faced her.

I was far too seriously startled by the suddenness with which this extraordinary apparition stood before me, in the dead of night and in that lonely place, to ask what she wanted. The strange woman spoke first.

"Is that the road to London?" she said.

I looked attentively at her, as she put that singular question to me. It was then nearly one o'clock. All I could discern distinctly by the moonlight was a colourless, youthful face, meagre and sharp to look at about the cheeks and chin; large, grave, wistfully attentive eyes; nervous, uncertain lips; and light hair of a pale, brownish-yellow hue. There was nothing wild, nothing immodest in her manner: it was quiet and self-controlled, a little melancholy and a little touched by suspicion; not exactly the manner of a lady, and, at the same time, not the manner of a woman in the humblest rank of life. The voice, little as I had yet heard of it, had something curiously still and mechanical in its tones, and the utterance was remarkably rapid. She held a small bag in her hand: and her dress – bonnet, shawl, and gown all of white – was, so far as I could guess, certainly not composed of very delicate or very expensive materials. Her figure was slight, and rather above the average height – her gait and actions free from the slightest approach to extravagance. This was all that I could observe of her in the dim light and under the perplexingly strange circumstances of our meeting.

What sort of a woman she was, and how she came to be out alone in the high-road, an hour after midnight, I altogether failed to guess. The one thing of which I felt certain was, that the grossest of mankind could not have misconstrued her motive in speaking, even at that suspiciously late hour and in that suspiciously lonely place.

"Did you hear me?" she said, still quietly and rapidly, and without the least fretfulness or impatience. "I asked if that was the way to London."

The **reading journey** can continue with a range of questions which could be distributed as appropriate. See how many pupils can access the **hardest question first**. Offer support as necessary:

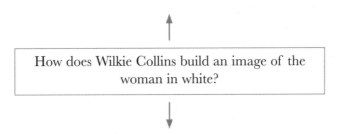

How does Wilkie Collins build an image of the woman in white?

Support questions could include:

🐛 Can you list how the woman looks to the narrator?

🐛 Use the illustration (on page 8) as a kind of close-up on the face. What does it make you think?

❦ Can you describe what she wears?

❦ Can you define any words you might not understand, like 'gait' or 'wistfully'?

❦ Describe in your own words a profile of the woman in white.

❦ How do we know whether the narrator feels threatened by the woman by the end of the passage?

❦ Will a chart support your thinking?

Physical features	Clothes	Overall impressions
Nervous uncertain lips	Small bag	Under pressure

Beyond the limit

Build in 'beyond the limit' reading and investigations at as early a stage as possible. The mystery genre is a popular area and it's vital to engage pupils' enthusiasm from any prior reading. Try some of these stories and detectives from the pioneering days of the mystery story:

❦ *The Moonstone* by Wilkie Collins (Sergeant Cuff)

❦ *The Hound of the Baskervilles* (see Unit 6) and other Sherlock Holmes stories by Sir Arthur Conan Doyle

❦ *Bleak House* by Charles Dickens (featuring Inspector Bucket)

❦ *Murders in the Rue Morgue* by Edgar Allan Poe (featuring Le Chevalier C. Auguste Dupin)

Other mysteries with a distinctive atmosphere include:

❦ *Noughts and Crosses* by Malorie Blackman

❦ The 'Artemis Fowl' series by Eoin Colfer

❦ The 'Hardy Boys' series by Franklin W. Dixon

❦ *Coraline* by Neil Gaiman

❦ *The Owl Service* by Alan Garner

❦ *Emil and the Detectives* by Erich Kästner

❦ *Why the Whales Came* by Michael Morpurgo

❦ *The Wind Singer* by William Nicholson

❦ The 'Swallows and Amazons' series by Arthur Ransome

❦ *The Silver Sword* by Ian Serraillier

Some of your pupils can **dig deeper** by launching investigations and explorations on related themes such as:

❦ How writers create mysterious characters (e.g. the Birdman in *Why the Whales Came*).

❦ How writers find original and convincing settings (e.g. a floral pattern on ancient dinner plates sets off the retelling of a Welsh myth in *The Owl Service*).

❦ How characters can be developed to solve mysteries in books which become a series.

❦ How *The Woman In White* might develop as a story – then see how much of it can be read!

Film clips from *The Woman in White* can be found on the internet – don't miss the one from the 1948 version directed by Peter Godfrey (http://www.tcm.com/mediaroom/video/275994/Woman-in-White-The-Movie-Clip-I-m-Afraid-I-m-Lost.html). Some of the old adaptations are better in terms of capturing an atmosphere closest to Collins's prose.

Wings to fly

The standard of the children's final written work will be partly conditioned by the richness of the 'beyond the limit' reading and partly by their engagement with the text, but all the pupils should enjoy writing a mystery!

Bob says ...

Choice is important. Some pupils may write a superb, fully sustained and lengthy mystery, but it's wise to advise them to maintain a simple focus or the possibilities are so huge that the writing can become unmanageable or intimidating. For this reason, you might want to limit the title to anything implying that a mystery is about to unfold, at least for some pupils.

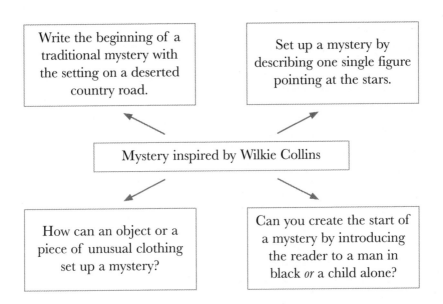

Write the beginning of a traditional mystery with the setting on a deserted country road.

Set up a mystery by describing one single figure pointing at the stars.

Mystery inspired by Wilkie Collins

How can an object or a piece of unusual clothing set up a mystery?

Can you create the start of a mystery by introducing the reader to a man in black *or* a child alone?

The advantage of maintaining a narrow focus is that the quality of the writing will be enhanced by imitating Collins, making us, the reader, shiver with apprehension! As your pupils have now done a taster draft, they are well placed to begin. Their plans could revolve around the anticipated response of the reader. A lot can be learnt from crafting phrases in a plan and then testing reactions with friends. Sometimes, I've found pupils enjoying the writing process but being quite unaware of the reaction of their words on others. Will the fictional mystery in their heads be well received by their friends when it's read? This unit should give them deeper practice in learning how words on a page start to connect with someone else's expectations.

Try peer marking on the relative effectiveness of each other's drafts using the following questions. Ask your pupils to predict each other's

denouement before it's been written. Predictions from other pupils' drafts or taster phrases will be enthusiastically received before final corrections and insertions.

❦ How will your friend's mystery develop?

❦ Did your friend's writing convey a shiver of fear or a moment of questioning?

❦ Was the character original?

❦ Did the character and setting complement one another?

It might be worth remembering this advice from Sir Arthur Conan Doyle in *The Adventures of Sherlock Holmes*: 'As a rule, the more bizarre a thing is the less mysterious it proves to be … a commonplace face is the most difficult to identify.' So, mystery does not have to come from the extraordinary. It's the questions readers are posed which start to trigger the tension!

A very rich whole-class **mini-plenary** will give you the chance to add any missing knowledge or to signpost routes to mastery. Get ready to appreciate and celebrate some original moments – the famous woman in white's appearance on the road to London should have started another quality text to quality writing journey!

Congratulations to Esme at Roch Community Primary School for succeeding in giving me a shiver of anticipation with this piece inspired by Wilkie Collins:

A gentle touch brought him back from his reverie. Whipping his head around he was startled to find a young woman.

A woman in white.

Her face shone, surrounded by a glowing aura. His mouth moved but no sound came out. Then she was gone, disappearing into the shadow of the dark caused by the bruised cloud that hovered above; waiting to let fly its thousand fleets of arrows.

That woman had seemed to recognise him ...

'Sir?' A voice cut through the silence of the lonely place.

Esme Pykett (Year 4)

This writing came after the teacher compared the opening of Neil Gaiman's *The Graveyard Book* with this extract from *The Woman in White*. The pupils also watched the 1948 film clip of the initial meeting between Walter Hartright and the woman in white.

Spooky Scientists!

The Phantom Coach by Amelia B. Edwards

Can you understand more about scientists in literature? How successfully can you create your own scientist in a piece of creative writing?

Access strategies

There is a fascinating history, going back to the oral tradition of storytelling, of writers featuring scientists on the verge of exciting discoveries. Sometimes, as with Merlin from the Arthurian legends, the scientist/wizard seems to be a wise, guiding spirit; in other stories, the deep knowledge they seek is threatening to humanity. Amelia B. Edwards was writing in Victorian times, and the eccentric scientist in *The Phantom Coach* has endured in a piece of writing which is rich in inference and **ambiguity**. It's great fun too!

Before revealing the extract from *The Phantom Coach*, your pupils will enjoy studying a painting by Hans Holbein the Younger called *The Ambassadors* (1533). You can find it easily on the internet. The objects in the painting will offer imaginative contrasts to the setting in the scientist's laboratory.

I suggest you crop the painting so that your pupils can focus on the objects only. Ask them to explore in groups what they are and what they might represent. (Watch out for the skull at the front, seen only from the side – an example of anamorphic perspective.) Now ask them to suggest what the two figures might look like in the full painting. You could restrict information about the title and the date of the artwork to add to the mystery. Then reveal the full painting!

This access strategy should help when your pupils are devising a spooky scientist and need to build in lots of detail to make it convincing. If you want another artist with suitable paintings to explore, try Joseph Wright of Derby: http://artuk.org/discover/artists/wright-of-derby-joseph-17341797. This will take their thinking into the eighteenth century.

Your pupils should now enjoy this encounter with a lost traveller in Amelia B. Edwards's 1864 ghost story. Amelia was an Egyptologist and was frequently asked by Charles Dickens to contribute stories to his magazines.

A traveller is lost in bad weather but finds shelter with an unusual man and his many strange possessions.

Smaller and less incongruous in its arrangements than the hall, this room contained, nevertheless, much to awaken my curiosity. The floor was carpetless. The whitewashed walls were in parts scrawled over with strange diagrams, and in others covered with shelves crowded with philosophical instruments, the uses of many of which were unknown to me. On one side of the fireplace stood a bookcase filled with dingy folios; on the other, a small organ, fantastically decorated with painted carvings of medieval saints and devils. Through the

Resource

half-opened door of a cupboard at the further end of the room I saw a long array of geological specimens, surgical preparations, crucibles, retorts, and jars of chemicals; while on the mantelshelf beside me, amid a number of small objects stood a model of the solar system, a small galvanic battery, and a microscope. Every chair had its burden. Every corner was heaped high with books. The very floor was littered over with maps, casts, papers, tracings, and learned lumber of all conceivable kinds.

I stared about me with an amazement increased by every fresh object upon which my eyes chanced to rest. So strange a room I had never seen; yet seemed it stranger still, to find such a room in a lone farmhouse amid those wild and solitary moors! Over and over again I looked from my host to his surroundings, and from his surroundings back to my host, asking myself who and what he could be? His head was singularly fine; but it was more the head of a poet than of a philosopher. Broad in the temples, prominent over the eyes, and clothed with a rough profusion of perfectly white hair, it had all the ideality and much of the ruggedness that characterizes the head of Ludwig von Beethoven. There were the same deep lines about the mouth, and the same stern furrows in the brow. There was the same concentration of expression.

Reading journeys

The passage tells us about the scientist's room and the visitor's impressions of his personality. Ask the children to use a **continuum line** to find any inference in the extract that the scientist's knowledge might be threatening or fascinating. The pupils should place the words or phrases which intrigue them on the line as appropriate. For example:

Fascination ⟵————————————⟶ Threat

Saints   Curiosity   Wild   Solitary   Devils

This should lead to considerable debate about the way language creates associations in our minds. Your pupils can then exploit what they learn in their own writing. How much they understand initially may depend on their prior reading experiences, so you might want to include some direct teaching to highlight the nuances of meaning in this extract.

For example, think of the implications building in these phrases:

❦ Philosophical instruments, the uses of many of which were unknown to me.

❦ Dingy folios.

❦ Every chair had its burden.

To the traveller, the room looks packed; the knowledge within it is outside his realm and seems very ancient. Through him, the reader begins to feel uneasy, uncertain and edgy.

Bob says ...

How will your pupils devise a scientist whose powers are ambiguous and whose role may verge on the frightening? Some of the young writers with whom I work love going overboard with spooky tales, mad scientists and ghost stories with dripping blood and gore! Do you have the same problem? The stimulus provided here should help your pupils to build detail and personality simultaneously and avoid the stereotypes sometimes associated with this genre.

You could **dig deeper** still by asking the pupils to list the objects, define them and state what they tell us about the scientist:

Object/ description	Definition	What do we learn?
Painted carvings	Ornate decorations on the organ	Musical? Gothic?
Crucible	Container that can be used in high temperatures	Doing dangerous experiments?

Beyond the limit

Select the most appropriate **link reading** for your pupils:

- *Jurassic Park* by Michael Crichton
- *The Tragical History of the Life and Death of Dr Faustus* by Christopher Marlowe
- The 'Northern Lights' series by Phillip Pullman (Mrs Coulter)
- *Frankenstein* by Mary Shelley
- *The Strange Case of Dr Jekyll and Mr Hyde* by Robert Louis Stevenson
- *Dracula* by Bram Stoker (see Unit 13 of *Opening Doors to Famous Poetry and Prose*)
- *The Time Machine* and *The Island of Dr Moreau* by H. G. Wells

Or compare and contrast some popular wizards:

- Gandalf from *The Lord of the Rings* by J. R. R. Tolkien
- Merlin from the Arthurian legends
- The wizard from *The Wonderful Wizard of Oz* by L. Frank Baum

Ask your keen and more able pupils to compile mad scientist/wizard profiles across various books to sift and sort their characteristics: Dr Jekyll compared with Mrs Coulter sounds interesting to me! Of course, using brief scenes from films of the above (many of which can be found on YouTube) will highlight similarities and differences.

There is a video reading of *The Phantom Coach* which does not focus on the extract studied here, but it does provide an atmospheric

version of the whole story: http://wn.com/the_phantom_coach_by_
amelia_edwards_%7C_classic_horror_storytime_with_otis_jiry.

Ask for predictions on how a phantom coach tale might develop and
how it might end. The full text of *The Phantom Coach* can be found at:
http://www.eastoftheweb.com/short-stories/UBooks/PhanCoac.
shtml.

Bob says ...

Philosophy for Children strategies often deepen engagement
and debate in English lessons. Your objectives will certainly
be addressed by exploring some of the big issues raised by
the reading:

* Is new scientific knowledge usually for the good of
  mankind?

* Is the pursuit of knowledge always to be encouraged?

* Should society put boundaries on what kind of science
  is allowed?

* How important is science as a subject at school?

H. G. Wells says in *The First Men in the Moon*: 'If we can possibly avoid
wrecking this little planet of ours, we will. But – there must be risks!
There must be. In experimental work there always are.' That might
help to start the discussions.

Wings to fly

Use the **radial questions** below to plan out some original writing with key questions to help.

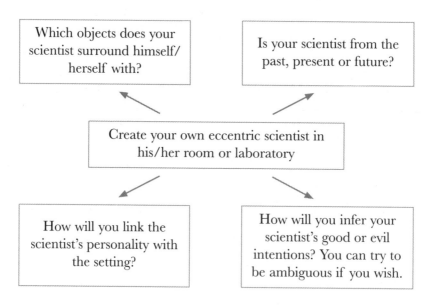

The following quirky ideas might appeal to some pupils:

❦ The contents of the dingy folios.

❦ Every chair had its burden. What was on them?

❦ How would you link this scene with a phantom coach?

❦ Create an eccentric female scientist in appropriate surroundings.

Perhaps most important of all:

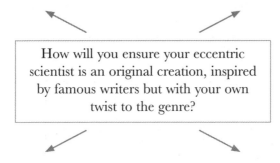

How will you ensure your eccentric scientist is an original creation, inspired by famous writers but with your own twist to the genre?

How many of your young writers are able to extend their character into a full tale? It would be unwise to hold them back, but a full narrative carries more of the traditional dangers of stereotyping – mad scientists, ghosts on castle walls and experiments producing strange shaped monsters! It is always originality rather than replication that we hope for, so getting into the habit of crafting their literary creation to fit a coherent story will produce the best responses.

I hope you will be inspired by this character creation from Jonathan at Churchfields Junior School in South Woodford:

The Scientist and his Room

As I stepped into his room, the cold, dingy air buffeted in my face. I looked around. The walls were bare and the floor had a threadbare rug. I glanced over and saw a cupboard filled with an array of books. I thought there were rats inside but I couldn't see clearly because the glass was very opaque because gas was seeping through. I turned to leave, but a pitch black silhouette blocked my retreat and then a voice spoke out.

'Why are you leaving now? You've only just come in but running away, well, that could be a sin.'

I spun on my heel and turned round to face him. He had cold, sad, mellow eyes which were dark blue but tinted green. He had perfect blond hair and did not have a lab coat but a fine, blue business coat and matching tie. He looked like he had been there for years, maybe he had, maybe not, who knows? He spoke with a soft voice like smooth butter.

'Welcome,' he paused, 'to my lab' and with a flourish of his coat I braced myself for the secret of his lab.

Jonathan Crossley (Year 4)

The Strongest Looking Brute in Alaska

That Spot by Jack London

How well can you write an effective denouement?

Access strategies

Jack London has become famous for his stories of the frozen wastes of the Yukon at the time of the Klondike Gold Rush. From 1896 to 1899, thousands of prospectors headed for the Klondike region of north-western Canada where gold had been discovered. *That Spot* is a short story written in 1908 about a dog the narrator would love to leave behind! It is not so well known as *Call of the Wild* or *White Fang*, but its lighter tone will be enjoyed by your pupils and the doors can then open to the longer stories.

This unit is an opportunity to use the ending of *That Spot* to make some transferable teaching points about the need to plan for a climax or a satisfying conclusion. I often find that the aspect young writers ignore the most is the one that the reader is anticipating from the start – the **denouement**!

Read with your class the start of the final section of *That Spot*:

And now for the sequel. You know what it is when a big river breaks up and a few billion tons of ice go out, jamming and milling and grinding. Just in the thick of it, when the Stewart went out, rumbling and roaring, we sighted Spot out in the middle. He'd got caught as he was trying to cross up above somewhere. Steve and I yelled and shouted and ran up and down the bank, tossing our hats in the air. Sometimes we'd stop and hug each other, we were that boisterous, for we saw Spot's finish. He didn't have a chance in a million. He didn't have any chance at all. After the ice-run, we got into a canoe and paddled down to the Yukon, and down the Yukon to Dawson, stopping to feed up for a week at the cabins at the mouth of Henderson Creek. And as we came in to the bank at Dawson, there sat that Spot, waiting for us, his ears pricked up, his tail wagging, his mouth smiling, extending a hearty welcome to us. Now how did he get out of that ice? How did he know we were coming to Dawson, to the very hour and minute, to be there on the bank waiting for us?

The more I think of that Spot, the more I am convinced that there are things in this world that go beyond science.

Try a **noticed/noted/not sure** sequence applied to this 'sequel':

- What do you notice which is surprising?
- What have you noted down which would make you think this is indeed moving to a conclusion as a story?

❦ What are you not sure about in terms of this passage being a denouement?

London signals the start of the end of his story with the short sentence setting up the sequel. This gives the pupils a very creative possibility for taster drafts:

❦ Write a brief, convincing earlier episode featuring Spot.

❦ Practise writing about the Yukon by taking some of the settings and using them in a descriptive piece.

❦ Look at the illustration (on page 37) and start developing a profile for Spot.

Assessment for learning will seem a natural process as your pupils feed back their drafts and gain advice from you and each other about how to shape the story using their settings. Above all, assess how they have worked backwards from the sequel to make assumptions about the narrative. They will love exploring new episodes for the incorrigible Spot! And why not ask them, en route, to use the internet to look up more about the Klondike Gold Rush.

Integrate appropriate 'beyond the limit' learning challenges for pupils at this early stage. For example, comparing this extract with the short story, *To Build A Fire* (1908), will deepen their comprehension and so the creative writing possibilities.

Bob says ...

*Including extension and enrichment at the end of a unit is the norm in some schools, but it makes sense to expect **link reading** and innovative writing from pupils who are ready, whenever they are ready.*

Is it essential in an enriched English curriculum that pupils who quickly master the basics can get extra practice on challenging objectives. In *Personalizing Learning* (2005), John West-Burnham and Max Coates describe deep learning as 'fundamentally concerned with the creation of knowledge, which the learner is able to relate to their own experience and use to understand new experiences and contexts'. Thus, all the 'beyond the limit' suggestions support the knowledge acquisition needed throughout the curriculum.

Reading journeys

Earlier in the story, London had reflected on Spot's personality.

He was a good-looker all right. When he was in condition his muscles stood out in bunches all over him. And he was the strongest-looking brute I ever saw in Alaska, also the most intelligent-looking. To run your eyes over him, you'd think he could outpull three dogs of his own weight. Maybe he could, but I never saw it. His intelligence didn't run that way. He could steal and forage to perfection; he had an instinct that was positively gruesome for divining when work was to be done and for making a sneak accordingly, and for getting lost and not staying lost he was nothing short of inspired. But when it came to work, the way that intelligence dribbled out of him and left him a mere clot of wobbling, stupid jelly would make your heart bleed.

There are times when I think it wasn't stupidity. Maybe, like some men I know, he was too wise to work. I shouldn't wonder

if he put it all over us with that intelligence of his. Maybe he figured it all out and decided that a licking now and again and no work was a whole lot better than work all the time and no licking. He was intelligent enough for such a computation. I tell you, I've sat and looked into that dog's eyes till the shivers ran up and down my spine and the marrow crawled like yeast, what of the intelligence I saw shining out. I can't express myself about that intelligence. It is beyond mere words. I saw it, that's all. At times it was like gazing into a human soul, to look into his eyes; and what I saw there frightened me [...]

As always, plan from the top with a hard, conceptual question to give all pupils practice in this kind of testing comprehension, but offer support questions as appropriate to those who need them. The 'Opening Doors' strategy relies on inclusion and learning challenges for all but with a consistently high pitch.

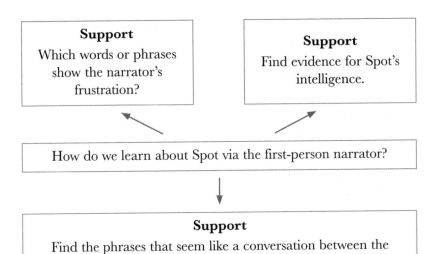

> **Support**
> Which words or phrases show the narrator's frustration?

> **Support**
> Find evidence for Spot's intelligence.

> How do we learn about Spot via the first-person narrator?

> **Support**
> Find the phrases that seem like a conversation between the narrator and the reader. How does the narrator feel?

Beyond the limit

Make links and comparisons between the extracts and the whole text reading of *Call of the Wild* and *White Fang*. Some pupils should be able to develop a fascinating author study of Jack London and his life. Ask the pupils to compare and contrast the different personalities he gives to his dogs and the very different owners who feature in the stories!

The whole story of *That Spot* is well worth reading with the class – it's very funny and will set up the quality writing expectations really well. There is an online version available at: http://www.pagebypage-books.com/Jack_London/That_Spot/That_Spot_p1.html. Compare it with the high tension in *To Build a Fire*: https://americanenglish. state.gov/resources/build-fire.

You won't be short of your own suggestions for dog tales but here are three very popular ones to start with:

- ❧ *Born to Run* by Michael Morpurgo
- ❧ *The One Hundred and One Dalmatians* by Dodie Smith
- ❧ *The Hundred-Mile-An-Hour Dog* by Jeremy Strong

For a super challenge, why not ask your most able pupils to justify their choice of most memorable canine creation by Jack London?

Wings to fly

Your pupils now have a deeper understanding of how to create a canine character in literature and an awareness of how important the denouement is to a story. Now let's put the two together for more 'wings to fly, not drills to kill'!

You could take the key connective or topic sentence, 'and now for the sequel', to guide your pupils' writing. Ask them to plan the sequel first or even write it before they write the beginning. This is not a sequel as in a separate story but a writing device to follow up a supposed resolution with a new revelation.

Bob says ...

In my writers' workshops, I have not found 'endings first' to be such an outrageous proposition. Many pupils will experiment in this way if they are given permission to do so. A traditional beginning, middle and end format helps some, but not all, pupils. Working out what will make your reader respond at the end of a narrative can support big picture planning.

The sequel approach may not be an option for everyone. The denouement could be planned using a number of visual shapes. Ask your pupils to choose their plot shape in groups and then consider improvements after peer discussions. These are a few of the shapes I have used:

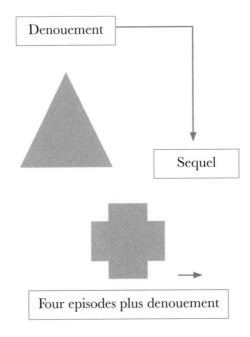

→ Denouement

The following ideas and titles should be good ones for the children to choose from to apply all the learning and knowledge they have acquired about how to write an excellent narrative:

- Write a Yukon tale (or indeed the tale of *That Spot*) from the dog's point of view. You could write about how he gets out of the ice in the incident from the first extract.

- 'His muscles stood out in bunches all over him'. Be very descriptive about your dog and the way you see it.

- Create a new episode in the Yukon for *That Spot*.

- Create your own mischievous or lazy dog who is also intelligent!

- 'A clot of wobbly, stupid jelly' shows a different side of Spot when there is work to be done. Can your story show a clever canine trying to 'make a sneak'?

- Write a dog tale which features a sequel to end it.

- 'I've sat and looked into that dog's eyes till the shivers ran up and down my spine'. Create a sinister dog in an appropriate setting.

Excellent responses will:

- Include a narrative which is well shaped and ends convincingly.

- Describe a very distinctive canine!

- Show relationship between the dog and its setting.

- Be written with the reader's response in mind.

Unit 4

Mr Knickerbocker's Notes

Rip Van Winkle by Washington Irving

Can you improve your narrative technique and ensure it supports the theme of your story?

Access strategies

For your pupils to learn more about narrative technique, try using Washington Irving's famous short story, *Rip Van Winkle*. The final section begins:

Resource 9

Postscript

The following are travelling notes from a memorandum book of Mr. Knickerbocker:

The Kaatsberg, or Catskill Mountains, have always been a region full of fable. The Indians considered them the abode of spirits, who influenced the weather, spreading sunshine or clouds over the landscape, and sending good or bad hunting seasons. They were ruled by an old squaw spirit, said to be their mother. She dwelt on the highest peak of the Catskills and had charge of the doors of day and night, to open and shut them at

the proper hour. She hung up the new moons in the skies and cut up the old ones into stars. In times of drought, if properly propitiated, she would spin light summer clouds out of cobwebs and morning dew and send them off from the crest of the mountain, flake after flake, like flakes of carded cotton, to float in the air; until, dissolved by the heat of the sun, they would fall in gentle showers, causing the grass to spring, the fruits to ripen, and the corn to grow an inch an hour.

I have always found this beguiling, beautiful and mysterious. It sends the imagination soaring across the Catskill Mountains and back to an ancient world of legend – and it reminds me of the awe-inspiring power of nature. But can this really be building towards an ending?

Ask your pupils to do a **prediction reversal**. Can they begin to work out what kind of narrative took place to lead to this ending? Try an evidence-based approach using strand-by-strand thinking:

❦ What genre is the story? How do you know?

❦ What kind of setting might the main story have if this is the start of the final section?

❦ Suggest three potential plot lines.

Ask the children to visualise plot possibilities on sugar paper and experiment with twists and turns in the narrative. See Unit 3 for some suggested plot shapes but, preferably, ask the pupils to invent their own.

A **taster draft** will enable deeper practice. Ask for a beginning along one of these lines:

❦ A further description of the squaw spirit's power.

❦ A scene on the Catskill Mountains.

❦ An example of bad weather when the spirit was displeased.

These will provide ways to play with words in a free and enjoyable way, allowing pupils to craft without constraint and experience brain **flow**. If done quickly after the planning the results should be very inventive. A **mini-plenary** can help to fill in any gaps in knowledge about the language, but those beginning to imitate Irving should have written some convincing drafts!

Reading journeys

Your pupils' curiosity should have been stimulated by the writing and their discussions, so feed them a further section which takes us to the end of *Rip Van Winkle*:

In old times, say the Indian traditions, there was a kind of Manitou or Spirit, who kept about the wildest recesses of the Catskill Mountains […]

The favorite abode of this Manitou is still shown. It is a great rock or cliff on the loneliest part of the mountains, and, from the flowering vines which clamber about it and the wild flowers which abound in its neighborhood, is known by the name of the Garden Rock. Near the foot of it is a small lake, the haunt of the solitary bittern, with water snakes basking in the sun on the leaves of the pond lilies which lie on the surface. This place was held in great awe by the Indians, insomuch that the boldest hunter would not pursue his game within its precincts. Once upon a time, however, a hunter who had lost his way penetrated to the Garden Rock, where he beheld a number of gourds placed in the crotches of trees. One of these he seized and made off with, but in the hurry of his retreat he let it fall among the rocks, when a great stream gushed forth, which washed him away and swept him down precipices, where he was dashed to pieces, and the stream made its way to the Hudson and continues to flow to the present day; being the identical stream known by the name of the Kaaters-kill.

Your pupils can learn more by responding to an open question approach with support offered as appropriate. Inventing lots of interesting questions will help.

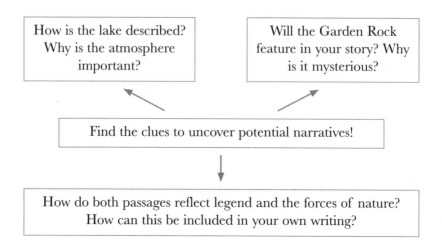

The idea is always to link the reading skills developed by reading literary texts with the journey to producing quality writing. In this way, opportunities to improve specific writing skills and experiment are built into the curriculum and into learning habits.

Beyond the limit

At an appropriate time, you will want to tell your pupils that Irving's story is called *Rip Van Winkle*. It is available here: http://www.bartleby.com/195/4.html. Written in 1819, it is very famous and tells the story of an American settler of Dutch descent whose journey on the Catskill Mountains leads to a meeting with strangely clad, mysterious folk. After drinking some of the local 'beverage', Rip sleeps for twenty years and misses the American Revolution!

You may be able to link *Rip Van Winkle* with other stories about encounters on mountains, time shifts and strange legends. Irving was one of the first authors to experiment with unusual narrative shifts and the ending is a way of making the events in the story seem authentic, although there is a wonderful tongue-in-cheek tone of humour throughout.

'A Tale of the Ragged Mountains' by Edgar Allan Poe will give your pupils more practice in understanding writing styles from the past. Poe was another literary pioneer attempting to break new ground in short story writing.

The idea of a Shangri-La, a beautiful place in the mountains, was furthered by James Hilton's 1933 novel *Lost Horizon*, and many fantasy tales and myths make much of what we might encounter in the hills.

More **link reading** on Native American legends will help too. There are many stories to browse on the internet, but for deeper delving why not recommend the pupils read some short sections of Henry Wadsworth Longfellow's famous narrative poem, *The Song of Hiawatha*.

Another link reading route might be with American writers:

- *The Old Man and the Sea* by Ernest Hemingway
- *The Legend of Sleepy Hollow* by Washington Irving (this contrasts well with *Rip Van Winkle*)
- *White Fang* by Jack London (see also Unit 3 on *That Spot*)
- *The Red Pony* and *The Pearl* by John Steinbeck

Bob says ...

Building in 'beyond the limit' work as a habit deepens our own knowledge base over time, not just that of our pupils. This is important. We may need to use only a small percentage of our expertise in front of the class, but that thickening base gives us the confidence to ask more searching questions, to cross-refer and to be creative in our interventions. We become activators of learning as well as facilitators.

Wings to fly

Enough should have been learnt about creative endings and narrative viewpoints to move your pupils towards the final stages of planning a narrative with an unusual ending like Irving's. It would make sense to exploit what they have absorbed about style and setting too, so why not try one of these ideas or titles:

❦ The Garden Rock

❦ Storm on the Catskills

❦ Devise your own fable of the Catskill Mountains.

❦ The Legend of Rip Van Winkle – Part 2!

❦ Write your own description of nature at work in the mountains.

❦ A lonely traveller passes by the lake where the water snakes bask. What happens next?

❦ 'She would spin light summer clouds out of cobwebs and morning dew'. Write a day in the life of the old squaw spirit.

Encourage an ending first strategy for the final planning. A mountain shaped story would be particularly appropriate! The **denouement** should be at the peak.

How can you encourage your pupils to plot deeper routes to secure improved writing and give further opportunities for mastery? It helps if you plan out your own excellence expectations which can also be shared with your pupils.

Excellent responses will include:

❦ A creative ending which still links with the main narrative.

❦ An imitation of Irving's creation of a mountain legend.

❦ An original character(s) related to the mountain setting.

❦ The mysterious sense of an ancient legend.

❦ Narrative flow.

❦ Spelling, punctuation and grammar to support style and meaning.

By its nature, excellent responses thinking plans from the top. This will help you to get more pupils to a higher standard. You can break down the success criteria into more manageable parts to clarify any areas you may wish to prioritise. So, an 'original character' could be explained as 'including something different' or 'narrative flow' as 'including connectives'. The responses are a guide to ambitious thinking, but the teachers with whom I work are, of course, intervening as appropriate to explain, enthuse and inspire!

As with much English work, the aim is for all pupils to learn more by the kind of reflection and risk-taking required here, so this is where programmes like Building Learning Power devised by Professor Guy

Claxton can boost achievement (see http://www.tloltd.co.uk/build-ing-learning-power/). Professor Claxton's pioneering work is helping schools to include learning to learn strategies in their curriculum and develop learning dispositions in much deeper and more effective ways. It's like exercising the mind.

All the units in this book require more flexing of imaginative muscles, and if this becomes a whole-school policy then it follows that progress will be improved. Schools that have invested in learning to learn will have more pupils who are more likely to excel with quirky or inventive tasks like these which require a relish in **new learning**!

Bob says ...

*Look back at the original images in the first extract – like 'she would spin light summer clouds out of cobwebs'. Encourage your pupils to feel the emotional and creative pull of these images to help them create their own original metaphors. This will develop their imaginative potential. If they visualise and articulate their **key images**, then that internal emotional response can start to be expressed in some remarkable writing inspired by Irving!*

I have worked with some pupils from The Grange Community Junior School in Farnborough, Hampshire, who loved the time slip theme and the idea of a legend set in the mountains. Here are some examples of how these themes helped their imaginations to thrive.

She felt lonely, life fading away as the skies darken and she rises up the mountain. What could stop it from happening? She rises from the ground, the world gets darker. Why is this happening? Then she drops to the ground, sad, unknown and forgotten. As she looks around the mountain, she sees the world in darkness.

Then, mysteriously, a gust of wind comes, it sounds like a message to change the world. But, the world remains as it was, dark, and she remains unknown and forgotten. Then again, a gust of wind comes and the same message comes. Then, with all her strength and power she blasts out a wind that blows away darkness ... she didn't know what to do ...

Ocean Guruny (Year 6)

She felt the power behind her eyes, then the destruction came. She used the wind to help her, fingers wanting to slash the sky like lightning, to make people flee in pain. She wanted people to see her power and worship her, like she always wanted. She sent dark clouds to represent her anger, the rain to be her tears of pain and she sent a thunder storm to ruin everything, a rumble from the core of the Catskill Mountains.

'Yes, yes,' she cackled to herself, deep in thought, 'destruction, destruction!'

She hated that colossal feeling of sorrow for her mother and father. She wanted the world to suffer because she had had to.

Laciejayne Rees (Year 6)

Unit 5

The Portrait of Doom

Tess of the D'Urbervilles by Thomas Hardy

How can objects be used imaginatively in creative writing?

Access strategies

Before reading a famous scene from Thomas Hardy's *Tess of the D'Urbervilles*, ask your pupils to reflect upon the portraits in the illustration.

❦ How would you describe each portrait?

❦ How do they make you feel?

❦ How do the portraits differ?

You could apply a **noticed/noted/not sure** sequence to go through thinking stages, using the final column for any open questions.

❦ What do you notice in the first minute of looking at the pictures?

❦ What is important enough to note down?

❦ What questions would you like to ask?

Ask your pupils to imagine the paintings are in an old manor house:

❦ Where are they hanging?

❦ What kind of atmosphere do the paintings exude?

If you search on the internet for 'Wool Manor' you will find pictures of the exact place on which Thomas Hardy based the scene which features the portraits, although it's called 'Wellbridge' in the story.

Ask the pupils to write a **taster draft**, inventing one or two characters who enter the manor house and see the paintings. Ask your pupils to use the question below to explore ways of linking their character with the setting.

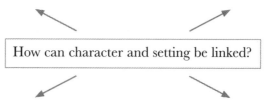

How can character and setting be linked?

Different support strategies are possible for those who are stuck. For example, the children could explore just the descriptive part of Hardy's scene at this stage to stimulate ideas and jump-start an understanding of the objective:

He looked up, and perceived two life-size portraits on panels built into the masonry. As all visitors to the mansion are aware, these paintings represent women of middle age, of a date some two hundred years ago, whose lineaments once seen can never be forgotten. The long pointed features, narrow eye, and smirk of the one, so suggestive of merciless treachery; the bill-hook nose, large teeth, and bold eye of the other, suggesting arrogance to the point of ferocity, haunt the beholder afterwards in his dreams.

Alternatively, you could search for visuals of Angel and Tess which would help to place your pupils' character in a Victorian time setting.

You are looking for the beginnings of a sophisticated link between the object – the painting or paintings – and the mood of the scene or the personality of the character. After making more teaching points, based on the relative success of the drafts, read your pupils the following longer extract.

Reading journeys

Hardy introduces the manor house in Chapter 34 of *Tess of the D'Urbervilles*: following her wedding to Angel Clare, Tess is taken by her new husband to the ancient house. From the start, the place has an unsettling feel to it, which is particularly reflected in the way Tess responds to paintings built into the masonry at the top of the stairs.

They drove by the level road along the valley to a distance of a few miles, and, reaching Wellbridge, turned away from the village to the left, and over the great Elizabethan bridge which gives the place half its name. […]

On entering they found that, though they had only engaged a couple of rooms, the farmer had taken advantage of their proposed presence during the coming days to pay a New Year's visit to some friends, leaving a woman from a neighbouring cottage to minister to their few wants. The absoluteness of possession pleased them, and they realized it as the first moment of their experience under their own exclusive roof-tree.

But he found that the mouldy old habitation somewhat depressed his bride. When the carriage was gone they ascended the stairs to wash their hands, the charwoman showing the way. On the landing Tess stopped and started.

'What's the matter?' said he.

'Those horrid women!' she answered, with a smile. 'How they frightened me.'

He looked up, and perceived two life-size portraits on panels built into the masonry. As all visitors to the mansion are aware, these paintings represent women of middle age, of a date some two hundred years ago, whose lineaments once seen can never be forgotten. The long pointed features, narrow eye, and smirk of the one, so suggestive of merciless treachery; the bill-hook nose, large teeth, and bold eye of the other, suggesting arrogance to the point of ferocity, haunt the beholder afterwards in his dreams.

'Whose portraits are those?' asked Clare of the charwoman.

'I have been told by old folk that they were ladies of the d'Urberville family, the ancient lords of this manor,' she said. 'Owing to their being builded into the wall they can't be moved away.'

The unpleasantness of the matter was that, in addition to their effect upon Tess, her fine features were unquestionably traceable in these exaggerated forms.

How can your pupils learn from Hardy about using an object in an imaginative way? How can they apply some of their ideas to their own sustained writing?

Try getting your pupils to continue this matrix to track the way the portraits start to establish a pattern of impending doom. Use the four segments as subheadings and ask your pupils to find ideas linked to each segment. You can help them by giving them the suggestions I've provided or see how well they can get started without additional help.

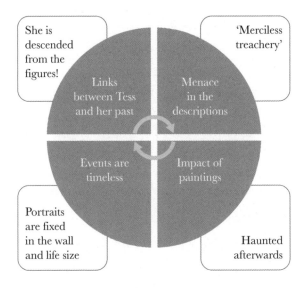

This will stimulate much deeper thinking, especially when your teaching points have been added too. Your pupils will learn how a famous writer has found a coherent way to suggest the influence of the past on Tess and Angel using the portraits as a powerful **motif**. Ask the children to discuss Hardy's name for the manor house – Wellbridge. Why might it be appropriate?

A question to test comprehension might be:

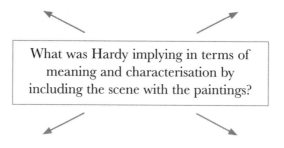

What was Hardy implying in terms of meaning and characterisation by including the scene with the paintings?

Beyond the limit

At any point in the process, you may wish to tell your pupils more about *Tess of the D'Urbervilles* and the life of Thomas Hardy. These links should help:

- ❦ Thomas Hardy Society – http://www.hardysociety.org/
- ❦ Poetry Foundation – http://www.poetryfoundation.org/bio/thomas-hardy

A few pupils might be ready to access Hardy's short stories or novels. If so, try *The Withered Arm* or *The Melancholy Hussar of the German Legion* from *Wessex Tales. Far from the Madding Crowd* is a terrific starting point for a first Hardy novel.

Hardy frequently explores the themes of past and present in his poetry, often using objects imaginatively. Perhaps ask some of your most able pupils to compare the style of the poems below with the depiction of the portraits in the extract, and then write a collection of short stories and/or poems around the theme of past and present.

❦ 'Old Furniture' (see Unit 17 in *Opening Doors to Famous Poetry and Prose*)

❦ 'The Clock-Winder'

❦ 'The Little Old Table'

❦ 'The Musical Box'

❦ 'The Photograph'

❦ 'To My Father's Violin'

If you want a more structured 'beyond the limit' opportunity, use the following poem which has a fascinating echo with the way Tess's past looms and leers over her. There is an original narrative waiting to be written by some of your pupils involving their own family face! It should provoke a lot of deeper thinking.

Heredity

I am the family face;
Flesh perishes, I live on,
Projecting trait and trace
Through time to times anon,
And leaping from place to place
Over oblivion.

The years-heired feature that can
In curve and voice and eye
Despise the human span
Of durance – that is I;
The eternal thing in man,
That heeds no call to die.

Thomas Hardy

Wings to fly

Routes to mastery in terms of writing about objects imaginatively
could be achieved in at least two ways: exploring the portrait idea
further or choosing a different object.

Here are some starter prompts if you want the children to focus on the portrait idea:

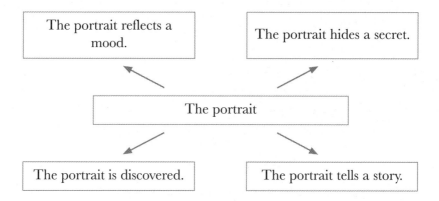

The portrait reflects a mood.		The portrait hides a secret.

The portrait

| The portrait is discovered. | | The portrait tells a story. |

Any of these could be developed into a full title. Here are some examples which the children could use as starting points:

❦ The hotel on the moors seemed comfortable and cosy – and then I saw the strange glow in the eyes of Lady Kilcullen's portrait.

❦ 'The portrait cannot be moved, madam, and I can show you the ancient document telling us why!'

You could find portraits on the internet to act as the central stimulus for a story – for example, *Whistler's Mother* by James McNeil Whistler (1871) is the kind of portrait which gives scope for debate, possibility and story-making.

Or you could make reference to two other famous narratives featuring paintings:

- 'The Oval Portrait' by Edgar Allan Poe in *Tales of Mystery and Imagination*
- *The Picture of Dorian Gray* by Oscar Wilde

If your pupils feel confined by the definition of 'portrait', then they can still apply their understanding of the objective by centring their tale around any painting or, in fact, any object. Hardy's poems demonstrate in various ways that an object is a lot more than just an item in a room – he often uses violins, furniture, coffins, clocks and photographs as a starting point for his work.

What matters most is that **excellent responses will**:

- Include objects which complement the narrative and the characterisation.
- Feature objects that help us to learn more about a theme or a character.
- Give the object an original role in the story.
- Integrate the object into the pattern and style of the overall story coherently and fluently.

Bob says ...

Hardy is the master of introducing layers of time into his stories like strata of rock on a cliff face. Your young writers can show how a portrait links the past to the present, but they could go even further and suggest different layers of the past all influencing every single thing we think and do today! How ambitious can they be?

Unit 6

The Hell Hound

The Hound of the Baskervilles
by Sir Arthur Conan Doyle

How effectively can you build tension in a narrative?

Access strategies

Read out this extract from *The Hound of the Baskervilles*. You could have lots of pictures of foggy scenes on a PowerPoint loop as you speak:

Resource 16

Every minute that white woolly plain which covered one-half of the moor was drifting closer and closer to the house. Already the first thin wisps of it were curling across the golden square of the lighted window. The farther wall of the orchard was already invisible, and the trees were standing out of a swirl of white vapour. As we watched it the fog-wreaths came crawling round both corners of the house and rolled slowly into one dense bank on which the upper floor and the roof floated like a strange ship upon a shadowy sea. Holmes struck his hand passionately upon the rock in front of us and stamped his feet in his impatience.

Try a **javelin** approach: aim high, aim fast and be ambitious! I antic-ipate some very exciting lessons where pupils move straight into some inventive writing. Don't tell them the passage is from *The Hound of the Baskervilles*; instead, ask them to invent a creature which is about to appear on the moors. Their idea must fit the description and atmos-phere of the extract, so their writing will also test their comprehension skills.

A brief **think, pair, share** can help to isolate promising ideas for discussion and unlikely ones to be dismissed – then let the pens flow!

In a **mini-plenary**, sift and sort the writing that best captures the setting and action. This should have engaged the imagination and attention ready for the full text which is from Chapter 14 of the book:

I have said that over the great Grimpen Mire there hung a dense, white fog. It was drifting slowly in our direction and banked itself up like a wall on that side of us, low but thick and well defined. The moon shone on it, and it looked like a great shimmering ice-field. […]

Resource 17

Every minute that white woolly plain which covered one-half of the moor was drifting closer and closer to the house. Already the first thin wisps of it were curling across the golden square of the lighted window. The farther wall of the orchard was already invisible, and the trees were standing out of a swirl of white vapour. As we watched it the fog-wreaths came crawling round both corners of the house and rolled slowly into one dense bank on which the upper floor and the roof floated like a strange ship upon a shadowy sea. Holmes struck his hand passionately upon the rock in front of us and stamped his feet in his impatience. [...]

There was a thin, crisp, continuous patter from somewhere in the heart of that crawling bank. The cloud was within fifty yards of where we lay, and we glared at it, all three, uncertain what horror was about to break from the heart of it. I was at Holmes's elbow, and I glanced for an instant at his face. It was pale and exultant, his eyes shining brightly in the moonlight. But suddenly they started forward in a rigid, fixed stare, and his lips parted in amazement. At the same instant Lestrade gave a yell of terror and threw himself face downward upon the ground. I sprang to my feet, my inert hand grasping my pistol,

Resource 18

my mind paralysed by the dreadful shape which had sprung out upon us from the shadows of the fog. A hound it was, an enormous coal-black hound, but not such a hound as mortal eyes have ever seen. Fire burst from its open mouth, its eyes glowed with a smouldering glare, its muzzle and hackles and dewlap were outlined in flickering flame. Never in the delirious dream of a disordered brain could anything more savage, more appalling, more hellish, be conceived than that dark form and savage face which broke upon us out of the wall of fog.

With long bounds the huge black creature was leaping down the track, following hard upon the footsteps of our friend. So paralysed were we by the apparition that we allowed him to pass before we had recovered our nerve.

Reading journeys

Ask your pupils to explore the question below and start sketching out what can be learnt from Conan Doyle's technique. They can invent questions and make comments in the white spaces and link this with highlightings or queries made about the text itself. **Text ownership** is vital to self-confidence. How many times, like me, have you said to a pupil, 'You can't find the answer by looking at the ceiling!' These kinds of reading journeys, exploring challenging texts, should help to build the habit of absorption in language and encourage active work towards deeper understanding.

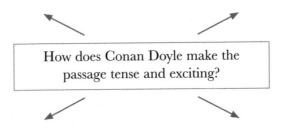

How does Conan Doyle make the
passage tense and exciting?

Support questions can be introduced as appropriate:

❦ How do we find out about Holmes's mood?

❦ What differences are there between Holmes's state of mind and
the narrator's?

❦ How is the hound described?

❦ How do the fog and cloud contribute to the tension?

❦ Explain and explore the importance of 'fog-wreaths', 'exultant',
'inert hand' and 'flickering flame'.

Central to the 'Opening Doors' strategy is that more pupils have the
chance to answer harder questions once they have engaged with the
texts, so I have suggested opportunities for complex conceptual thinking first with easier questions seen as support. You may wish to include
further access questions to build confidence, such as asking for a comment on how adjectives like 'savage' and 'dark' tell us more.

This is also where spelling, punctuation and grammar can be taught
in context. While your pupils are in an enquiring frame of mind, you
can point out the double 'z' of 'muzzle', the connective phrase 'at the
same instant' or the commanding tone of the sentence beginning

'Never in the delirious dream'. It makes a lot more sense than teaching using discrete exercises because pupils can see how decisions about spelling, punctuation and grammar affect meaning.

Professor Debra Myhill has researched how grammar can be taught in context. Her report, 'Words with Ways: How Grammar Supports Writing' (2015), will be a helpful addition to your thinking. In it she describes how grammar can be made explicit 'at a point in the teaching sequence which is relevant to the focus of learning'.

Look for some of the following points from your pupils focusing particularly on evidence provided on language effect.

Excellent responses will:

❦ Include examples of the way the fog adds a haunting sense of the unseen (e.g. the alliteration of 'white woolly plain').

❦ Explain how the level of detail adds to the tension (e.g. 'fog-wreaths came crawling round both corners').

❦ Stress how the uncertainty builds via characters and setting.

❦ Describe how Holmes is shown as being excited and impatient.

❦ Explain how the narrator's fear translates itself to the reader with a series of clauses focusing directly on the ferocious hound.

There is likely to be a vital learning session where the pupils report back progress on their **white space thinking** exercise. At this point, you can introduce the deeper knowledge needed on areas where even the most able may struggle. However, the support questions and access strategies should have helped the comprehension of those of lower ability too.

Bob says ...

In all my work with schools on 'Opening Doors', I have been encouraged by the feedback that lower ability pupils love the creative opportunities afforded by the extracts. You should find that they respond well to ambitious questions as long as the access strategies have succeeded. Get them hooked with the excitement: the mist, the moors, the hound and Holmes himself!

Beyond the limit

Try comparing *The Hound of the Baskervilles* with other famous literary canines:

- *The Incredible Journey* by Sheila Burnford
- *Oliver Twist* by Charles Dickens (an internet image search will reveal lots of famous illustrations of Bill Sikes's loyal bull terrier, Bull's Eye, who is brutally treated by Sikes)
- *That Spot* by Jack London (see Unit 3)
- *Call of the Wild* and *White Fang* by Jack London
- *The Hundred and One Dalmatians* by Dodie Smith

Ask your pupils to deepen their study by sketching out the very different ways these authors have used dogs to create tension or even to steer the whole story.

Alternatively, some pupils might like to explore the kind of traditional atmosphere of adventure and mystery they have tasted in this story. In which case, try dipping into these texts by pioneers of tales about detectives, spies, chases and foreign intrigues:

- *The Thirty-Nine Steps* by John Buchan
- Detective stories featuring Hercule Poirot and Miss Marple by Agatha Christie
- *The Moonstone* and *The Woman in White* by Wilkie Collins
- *The Lost World* and the Sherlock Holmes stories by Sir Arthur Conan Doyle
- *Rogue Male* by Geoffrey Household
- *Journey to the Centre of the Earth* by Jules Verne (see Unit 10 of *Opening Doors to Famous Poetry and Prose*)

A full version of *The Hound of the Baskervilles* is available at: http://www.gutenberg.org/files/2852/2852-h/2852-h.htm.

Wings to fly

Ask your pupils to write down three important things they have learnt so far about creating tension. I wonder if they will include:

- Building a setting which infers uncertainties.
- Developing character and setting together.
- Deciding on how much to imply and how much to tell.
- Delivering a few sustained sentences of either revelation, horror or surprise to release the tension.

Having learnt from Conan Doyle's example, it's time for the children to put *The Hound of the Baskervilles* into the context of other **link reading** about tension and plan something original to write.

Bob says ...

Of course, great writers play with our expectations, break the rules and take risks, so there are no hard and fast rules or creativity would become conformity!

Ask the pupils to try one of these ideas:

- ❦ Create your own hell hound but in a different setting.

- ❦ Build tension for a different event set on Grimpen Mire.

- ❦ Use 'fog-wreaths' as the centre of your narrative which will provoke uncertainty in the reader.

- ❦ Continue the passage to reveal more about the hell hound.

- ❦ The path across the mire or bog will be covered by fog in thirty minutes. Three people are still out there. What happens next?

Your pupils might like to try a **mind link** where they relate something known with something out of their experience. Ask them to think of a moment of tension which could be centred around mounting uncertainty. If they cannot come up with an example, try the list below:

- ❦ Are you going to be late for a train?

- ❦ Can the team you support still win the game with five minutes left?

- ❦ Your mobile phone does not work and your parents are expecting you to call them ...

Everyone has experienced tension so it is a relatable feeling to jump-start the creativity! A debate in class or a role play can now support the writing as the children's imagination goes into more uncharted territory. In *Daniel Deronda*, George Eliot says: 'Here undoubtedly lies the chief poetic energy – in the force of the imagination that pierces or exalts the solid fact.'

Finally, enjoy the imaginative power and tension building of Owen's writing:

The Daunting Footsteps

As the thin coils of fog rolled toward me, I could make out a faint sound of footsteps coming closer when suddenly they stopped. Silence. The wind howled along the horizon. I stepped back; I could barely see the church now. It was engulfed by the great wall of fog. The willow a few feet in front of me stood crooked with branches spreading in every way possible. I could make out the crisp, thin footsteps. Only a few metres in front of me, I could make out a dark shape. It looked like it was coming closer and closer …

Owen Lee, Fort Hill Community School (Year 7)

Unit 7

Sinister Spaces

Metamorphosis and *The Castle* by Franz Kafka

Do you leave your reader enough space between the lines to ask questions about your story? This unit has been designed to help pupils explore a writing technique where the reader is being encouraged to ask questions and may not get all the answers!

Access strategies

Give half the class an envelope containing this opening from Franz Kafka's *Metamorphosis*:

One morning Gregor Samsa woke in his bed from uneasy dreams and found he had turned into a huge verminous insect. He lay on his hard shell-like back, and when he raised his head slightly he saw his rounded brown underbelly, divided into a series of curved ridges.

Give the other half this quote from the beginning of *The Castle* by the same author:

It was late evening when K. arrived. The village lay deep in snow. Nothing could be seen of the Castle Hill, it was hidden in mist and darkness, and not even the faintest gleam of light indicated the great castle there.

Allow your pupils about eight minutes to list as many questions as possible that they would like to ask about their extract. They should write the questions on sticky notes and then spend another five minutes placing what they consider to be their best question at the centre of a hexagon shaped chart like this:

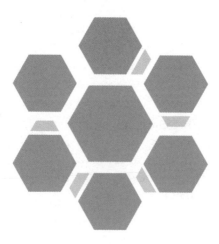

The idea is to encourage them to make decisions about the most incisive questions, which then get placed in the middle. When they write, they should aim to write something which prompts just as many fascinating questions in their readers.

Now, team up a *Metamorphosis* expert with a *Castle* expert! The paired partners can take it in turns to be a **question master**. The text, which is of course unseen to their partner, should now be revealed and explained, the questioning exercise having equipped the pupils to be teachers as well as question masters. The **talking partners** then need to invent further questions and answer the ones devised.

A **taster draft** is now needed to exploit the learning and interest and channel this into some quality writing! Ask each pupil to write the next paragraph of the text on which they did *not* do the questioning exercise. This should be done in silence for about fifteen minutes with an emphasis on leaving 'spaces' for the reader to hypothesise and for meaning to be inferred but not stated.

Bob says ...

You should find that having to write a continuation for the text they did not study will support the pupils' participation as a talking partner and certainly enhance their listening skills. If you can follow a **listen, learn, apply** sequence in group work, this should sharpen their conversations as each pupil must demonstrate learning after the group session. Hence the phrase 'productive group work', where the process of quality talk supports the outcome of the written work as well as being an outcome in itself.

To summarise, this exercise could be organised along these lines:

- Envelopes handed out with different Kafka extracts – half the class with *Metamorphosis* and the other half with *The Castle*.
- Each half of the class devises questions based on their own extract.
- 'Experts' now take their extract and questions to teach someone who studied the other extract.
- Swap over.
- Write a brief continuation to practise the skill of setting up possibilities.

Feedback should concentrate on whether a draft has told us too much, too little or has included specific ways of capturing our attention. Now offer a little more of Kafka which will deepen the pupils' comprehension and understanding.

Metamorphosis

One morning Gregor Samsa woke in his bed from uneasy dreams and found he had turned into a huge verminous insect. He lay on his hard shell-like back, and when he raised his head slightly he saw his rounded brown underbelly, divided into a series of curved ridges, on which the bedding could scarcely stay in place and was about to slip off completely. His numerous legs, which were pitifully thin relative to the rest of his body, wriggled helplessly in front of his eyes.

'What has happened to me?' he thought. It was not a dream. His room, quite adequate for one person though rather too small, was there as usual with its familiar four walls. Spread out on the table was a collection of samples of material he had unpacked – Samsa was a travelling salesman – and above it hung the picture he had recently cut out of an illustrated magazine and set in a handsome gilt frame. It showed a lady with a fur hat and wrap sitting upright and holding out towards the viewer a heavy fur muff which covered the whole of her forearm.

The Castle

It was late evening when K. arrived. The village lay deep in snow. Nothing could be seen of the Castle Hill, it was hidden in mist and darkness, and not even the faintest gleam of light indicated the great castle there. For a long time K. stood on the wooden bridge leading from the main road to the village, looking up into the apparent emptiness.

Then he set out to find lodgings for the night. At the inn they were still up; the landlord was taken aback and disturbed by the late arrival of a guest, but although he had no rooms free he was willing to let K. sleep on a straw mattress in the parlour, which K. found acceptable.

Resource 23

Reading journeys

Try a reversal of the usual order of questions. The pupils already have evaluative links in their minds as a result of the access exercise done earlier, so this time start with broader linking strategies:

❧ How does the mystery of the castle differ from the shock of Samsa's awakening in the way they are described?

❧ Are there any similarities or differences between K. and Samsa?

Reflection using this kind of breadth should then support in-depth thinking about each individual text:

Metamorphosis

1. How does the description of Samsa's body help to make the reader believe in such a shock opening? Which phrases are the most effective?

2. What is the contrast between the atmosphere of the room in paragraph two and the 'verminous' insect Samsa has become in paragraph one?

3. What does 'metamorphosis' mean? Could it be a symbol or a metaphor?

Excellent responses will:

- Include the effect of exact details like 'curved ridges' compared with the slippery bedding. It's an insect and yet it's a man! The 'eyes' looking at the body enforce this.

- Include an explanation of the way 'pitifully thin' and 'helpless' suggest vulnerability.

- Show how we pick up images of Samsa through what Kafka chooses to mention. The scene is described using adjectives and a visual scanning of the room.

The Castle

1. What does Kafka tell us about the castle and how does he do it?

2. What is unusual or unexpected about the brief paragraph in which K. is trying to find lodgings?

Excellent responses will:

❧ Explore the build-up of tension. It is a castle on a hill and a 'great' castle, yet we cannot see it. There is 'apparent emptiness'. 'Apparent' suggests we cannot be sure and so the mystery deepens. The short sentence mentions the snow but no more. Our imagination fills in the gaps.

❧ Discuss the burst of emotion in one phrase – 'taken aback' – and how this introduces a different tone.

❧ Explore the use of the straw mattress image and discuss how no room at the inn sets up an intriguing notion of who K. is.

❧ Include an exploration of how the use of the capital letter only in a name, K., may suggest someone who is hard to identify. This may link with the castle description as it's also hard to see and understand.

Bob says ...

*For pupils to explore an objective in depth there needs to be scope in the text for **new learning** about language, style and meaning. It's a good idea to prepare quite detailed success criteria, which is why I always recommend 'excellent responses will', as it's not just a mark scheme but a way in which schools have been working with me to* *deepen teachers' knowledge. Some **didactic teaching** may be necessary because there is new knowledge to impart. The more complicated the text, the more new learning may take place. It's an opportunity!*

For those who are stuck and need support, try this kind of chart:

Description of Samsa	Insect images
Uneasy dreams	Shell-like back
Salesman	

Description of K.	Castle images
K. is a traveller	Great
Reflects on the castle	

Beyond the limit

Franz Kafka was born in Prague in 1883, and his work is generally read by adults rather than children. He has a reputation for writing about strange and frightening situations where authority appears face-less. However, I have found that pupils love the 'verminous insect' episode in particular. It sparks their imagination and they can be taught a lot about writing with the readers' response in mind. They might like to find out more about this famous writer by looking at this website: http://www.kafka-online.info/.

Other **core reading** could be via writers who like experimenting with unusual images:

- ❦ *The Sleeper and the Spindle, Coraline* and *The Graveyard Book* by Neil Gaiman
- ❦ 'The Tell-Tale Heart' and 'A Descent into the Maelström' by Edgar Allan Poe (see Unit 15 of *Opening Doors to Famous Poetry and Prose*)
- ❦ *The Invisible Man* by H. G. Wells
- ❦ *Face* by Benjamin Zephaniah

In particular, point your pupils in the way of William Nicholson's 'Wind on Fire' trilogy, where one of the main characters, Kestrel Hath, rebels against exams and the Chief Examiner has the power to punish the whole family! This may be a very rich reading experience to echo the feeling of powerlessness which Samsa and K. seem to share. For deeper thinking around *The Castle*, paintings by Pieter Bruegel the Elder may help, especially *Hunters in the Snow* (1565).

Wings to fly

The taster draft earlier should have stimulated a lot of enthusiasm. Now you can explore different routes to sustained and imaginative writing.

The maze route

Pupils choose a route with your advice – offer different angles on a similar theme to reach the centre of the maze (i.e. achieving the objectives suggested in the excellent responses will list) by a chosen path.

- Try to describe how Gregor Samsa does the following in his insect body:
  - Get out of bed.
  - Leave his bedroom.
  - Travel to the office.

- Describe how a different character does the above but he/she has woken as a creature other than an insect!

- Focus on just one of Samsa's practical activities, such as making breakfast!

The javelin route

Javelin tasks are for writers who love the challenge thrown high so they can express fast, creative responses:

- Show the mist clearing gradually and dawn breaking so the reader can learn more about the castle.

- Write a first person account of either K. or Samsa's first hour of the day.

❧ Pick a well-known image with very particular associations but use
it to write an original story. Like Kafka, leave some things
unexplained and let the reader fill in the gaps imaginatively.
Suggestions of images might be:

- A church.
- An outsider.
- A barren marshland.
- An underground scene.
- The open sea.

The meandering river

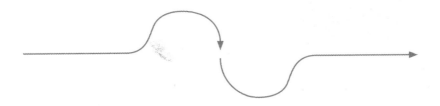

This is an exciting challenge for those who are ready for it. Here, the
shape of the story must have at least two surprise twists to it. The
pupils should aim to imply meaning rather than tell the reader too
much. Encourage them to experiment and take risks.

Here is the title: A Day in the Life of a Faceless Person. The pupils
can interpret this however they wish!

All these suggestions share similar and very ambitious success criteria:

Excellent responses will:

❦ Demonstrate a sinister atmosphere.

❦ Include space for the reader to ask questions.

❦ Incorporate **ambiguity** of meaning.

❦ Use spelling, punctuation and grammar to enhance meaning.

Unit 8

The Mirror and the Window

Wuthering Heights by Emily Brontë

Can you find creative ways to express a character's powerful emotions?

Access strategies

Read out the following extract from Chapter 12 of Emily Brontë's *Wuthering Heights* but don't tell your pupils anything about the background:

Resource 24

"Don't *you* see that face?" she enquired, gazing earnestly at the mirror.

And say what I could, I was incapable of making her comprehend it to be her own; so I rose and covered it with a shawl.

"It's behind there still!" she pursued, anxiously. "And it stirred. Who is it? I hope it will not come out when you are gone! Oh! Nelly, the room is haunted! I'm afraid of being alone!"

I took her hand in mine, and bid her be composed, for a succession of shudders convulsed her frame, and she *would* keep straining her gaze towards the glass.

"There's nobody here!" I insisted. "It was *yourself*, Mrs. Linton; you knew it a while since."

"Myself!" she gasped, "and the clock is striking twelve! It's true, then; that's dreadful!"

Her fingers clutched the clothes, and gathered them over her eyes. I attempted to steal to the door with an intention of calling her husband; but I was summoned back by a piercing shriek. The shawl had dropped from the frame.

"Why, what *is* the matter?" cried I. "Who is coward now? Wake up! That is the glass – the mirror, Mrs. Linton; and you see yourself in it, and there am I, too, by your side."

Trembling and bewildered, she held me fast, but the horror gradually passed from her countenance; its paleness gave place to a glow of shame.

"Oh, dear! I thought I was at home," she sighed. "I thought I was lying in my chamber at Wuthering Heights. Because I'm weak, my brain got confused, and I screamed unconsciously. Don't say anything; but stay with me. I dread sleeping, my dreams appal me."

An **inform and infer** chart will support your pupils' thinking. What do we learn from the passage which could be regarded as factual information? What do we learn which can be inferred and may imply meaning and emotion, but which may be less overt?

Inform	Infer
Mrs Linton is looking at the mirror.	Is Mrs Linton paranoid?
She is ill.	

As your pupils explain and explore the passage, ask them these questions:

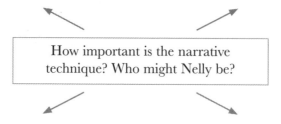

How important is the narrative technique? Who might Nelly be?

Use the idea of someone, unwell and confined to bed, who is disturbed by what he or she sees in the mirror. Ask the pupils to write a **taster draft** which has the aim of using a mirror to show a disturbed state of mind. Assessment for learning should focus around those ideas with the most potential for originality. How can they be developed?

Whenever it seems appropriate, tell your pupils more about Emily Brontë and *Wuthering Heights* and link in the **core reading** from 'beyond the limit'.

Catherine Linton has grown up at Wuthering Heights as Catherine Earnshaw, the daughter of the owner and sister of Hindley. Her father brings home a homeless boy from the streets of Liverpool called Heathcliff. Catherine and Heathcliff become soul mates but Heathcliff is driven out by Hindley, who becomes the owner of Wuthering Heights when his father dies. Catherine is tempted by the relative sophistication of Edgar Linton who lives nearby at Thrushcross Grange. She marries him, but can she ever really leave her feelings for her soul mate behind?

Read the next extract to satisfy your pupils' growing curiosity (it is also from Chapter 12 and features Catherine and Nelly Dean). Ask them to compare the use of the mirror with the opened casement window.

"Oh, I'm burning! I wish I were out of doors – I wish I were a girl again, half savage and hardy, and free … and laughing at injuries, not maddening under them! Why am I so changed? why does my blood rush into a hell of tumult at a few words? I'm sure I should be myself were I once among the heather on those hills … Open the window again wide, fasten it open! Quick, why don't you move?"

"Because I won't give you your death of cold," I answered.

"You won't give me a chance of life, you mean," she said sullenly. "However, I'm not helpless yet, I'll open it myself."

And sliding from the bed before I could hinder her, she crossed the room, walking very uncertainly, threw it back, and bent out, careless of the frosty air that cut about her shoulders as keen as a knife.

I entreated, and finally attempted to force her to retire. But I soon found her delirious strength much surpassed mine (she *was* delirious, I became convinced by her subsequent actions and ravings).

There was no moon, and every thing beneath lay in misty darkness; not a light gleamed from any house, far or near; all had been extinguished long ago; and those at Wuthering Heights were never visible … still she asserted she caught their shining.

"Look!" she cried eagerly, "that's my room with the candle in it, and the trees swaying before it … and the other candle is in Joseph's garret … Joseph sits up late, doesn't he? He's waiting till I come home that he may lock the gate … Well, he'll wait a while yet. It's a rough journey, and a sad heart to travel it; and we must pass by Gimmerton Kirk, to go that journey! We've braved its ghosts often together, and dared each other to stand among the graves and ask them to come … But Heathcliff, if I dare you now, will you venture? If you do, I'll keep you. I'll not lie there by myself; they may bury me twelve feet deep, and throw the church down over me, but I won't rest till you are with me … I never will!"

Reading journeys

Stretch and challenge your pupils' minds by encouraging them to explore the principal evaluative question below. Use the questions surrounding the main one as prompts for those pupils who are stuck.

Excellent responses will:

❧ Discuss her passion and delirium – the use of exclamation marks, rapid utterances and broken speech.

❧ Explore the narrator's rationalising contrasts with Catherine's vision of Wuthering Heights.

❧ Discuss her personal address to Heathcliff.

❧ Discuss the detail in Catherine's childhood memories with proper nouns.

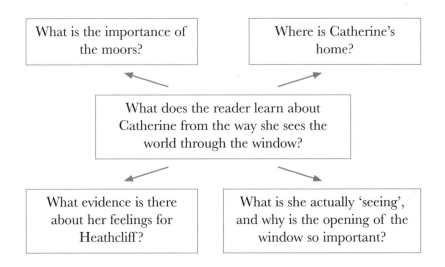

What is the importance of the moors?	Where is Catherine's home?

What does the reader learn about Catherine from the way she sees the world through the window?

What evidence is there about her feelings for Heathcliff?	What is she actually 'seeing', and why is the opening of the window so important?

Catherine says she will not rest until Heathcliff is with her. Yet, she has married Edgar Linton and will shortly die in childbirth. So, does the window act as an opening out to the truth, or is she merely delirious, sick and paranoid? Try linking this extract with the scene in Chapter 3 narrated by the traveller, Lockwood, who stays at Wuthering Heights (chronologically much later in the story), only to hear strange cries in the night and then clutch a child's frozen hand through the window and rub it brutally across the broken glass! It appears to be Catherine, begging to come home! So, reading the full text rewards the reader with a direct connection between Catherine's promise leaning out of the casement window with the sensational beginning to the story.

Bob says ...

Emily Brontë is one of the first novelists to experiment with time shifts and varied narrators. It should give your pupils ideas about experimenting with their own writing. In **Aspects of the Novel**, E. M. Forster says that 'a novel is a story, and a story is a narrative of events arranged in time sequence'. He says 'in a novel there is always a clock. The author may dislike his clock. Emily Brontë in **Wuthering Heights** tried to hide hers.' Forster is saying that writers will end up with a narrative – the clock is always ticking, taking us on to the next page – but authors can manipulate that 'clock' to suit their own ends. Can your pupils tell their stories using unusual narrative techniques?

Beyond the limit

You will find other passages from *Wuthering Heights* useful in deepening understanding and building writing ideas.

- There is a plot summary at: http://www.wuthering-heights.co.uk/summary.php.

- The full text is available at: http://literature.org/authors/bronte-emily/wuthering-heights/index.html.

- You will also find plenty of information about the Brontës at the Brontë Society website: https://www.bronte.org.uk/.

- You can cross-refer this text with Unit 9 which features 'Mementos' by Charlotte Brontë.

An idea with which the most able could **dig deeper** would be to compare the atmosphere of Wuthering Heights with that of Thornfield in *Jane Eyre* by Charlotte Brontë, or the rather preternatural longings of Heathcliff and Catherine with Rochester's growing affection for Jane Eyre. The theme of class difference and class barriers is common to both. Unit 14 on *Jane Eyre* in *Opening Doors to Famous Poetry and Prose* will also be useful for cross-reference.

For some pupils, graphic novels and film clips will support comprehension and engagement. However, always make sure your graphic novel selection uses the original text. (A number of schools use the Classical Comics editions.) There are plenty of film versions freely available on YouTube. Why not find this particular episode but compare different productions for a much richer evaluative experience?

The ghastly mirror scene may set up further comparative ideas using:

❦ *Through the Looking Glass* by Lewis Carroll

❦ 'Mirror' by Sylvia Plath

❦ Fairy tales like *Sleeping Beauty*

❦ The Greek myth of Narcissus looking at his own reflection

How many different ways can your pupils find to use a mirror in their creative writing in clever, fantastical or original ways? What can it tell us about their characters?

Wings to fly

It's time to develop those earlier taster drafts into some memorable creative writing! I have grouped possible titles into those stimulated by the mirror scene and those inspired by the opened window.

Whatever the title, encourage your pupils to look for creative ways to express emotion. The writing might be a soliloquy, a description or a fantasy, but it should express the character's feelings in ways which give the reader information and also more subtle meanings to dig for. Take your lessons from Emily Brontë!

❦ The mirror:

  ⚜ My Mood Mirror: A Diary

  ⚜ Last Lot at the Auction: The Eighteenth Century Mirror

  ⚜ The Mirror in the Attic Always Had a Huge, Brown Cloth Over It ...

  ⚜ A Liquid Mirror: A Journey Through My Reflection

- Mirror, Mirror On the Wall, Who Will Be the Oldest of Us All?
- The open window:
  - The View of Childhood
  - Storms in My Head and in the Sky!
  - Night Sky from the Casement
  - A Window of Opportunity
  - Not a Light Gleamed from Any House – Except One!

Some of your ambitious writers might like to link the mirror image with the open window scene:

- Looking In and Looking Out: The Mirror and the Window

Bob says …

Link back to the previous thinking about E. M. Forster's notion of changing your narrative 'clock'. Emily Brontë uses a number of narrators in **Wuthering Heights**. *Ask your pupils to think carefully about how the story is told. Whose perspective matters? Is your narrator writing in the first person? Could they include two perspectives on the same event or image?*

Part 2

Opening doors
to poetry

Resource 2

All in This House
is Mossing Over

From 'Mementos' by Charlotte Brontë

How well can you create a haunting atmosphere of decay?

Access strategies

Start by looking at the illustration.

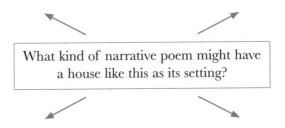

What kind of narrative poem might have
a house like this as its setting?

Use **evidence circles** to prompt reasons and further questions.
Ensure pupils link answers with their previous **reading journeys** or
film associations.

Now, if you are wondering how to exploit the genuinely sinister feel of Charlotte Brontë's poem with all abilities in mind, why not try a dramatic reading of **stanzas** five and six first?

Resource

> And outside all is ivy, clinging
> To chimney, lattice, gable grey;
> Scarcely one little red rose springing
> Through the green moss can force its way.
>
> Unscared, the daw, and starling nestle,
> Where the tall turret rises high.
> And winds alone come near to rustle
> The thick leaves where their cradles lie.

Then try what I call **chart attack** where the pupils list, in just three minutes in total, words or phrases on a theme in the left-hand column and then invent opposite ideas for the right-hand column. For example, ask pupils to list what is 'outside' and then try to find phrases to anticipate what might be inside.

Outside	Inside
Ivy clings to chimneys, gables, etc.	A fireplace with only ashes
A tall turret	

An open question for all deepens thinking:

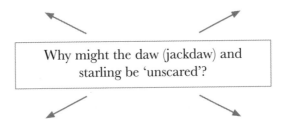

Why might the daw (jackdaw) and starling be 'unscared'?

Now, ask your pupils to write a **taster draft** about the inside of the house (which is obviously a grand one) in a couple of stanzas or in prose. This is a taster of what is to come – a chance to shine early in the process. It's great fun too! You could give further prompts about the likely atmosphere inside the grand house if you wish – for example, 'high ceilings with fractured beams'.

Bob says ...

Sometimes pupils write so many long drafts that they lose momentum and don't necessarily write more effectively. In contrast, a taster draft will deepen the engagement and satisfy the need to write, which sometimes gets delayed for too long in literacy lessons. Taster drafts can have a huge impact as long as you facilitate some rich discussions on what is exceptional and how each draft could be improved. This kind of assessment for learning should lead to clear teaching points – for example, about using the right kind of metaphor or adjective.

All your pupils should now read this extract from the early part of the poem with you in a totally immersed way.

From 'Mementos'

I scarcely think, for ten long years,
A hand has touched these relics old;
And, coating each, slow-formed, appears,
The growth of green and antique mould.

All in this house is mossing over;
All is unused, and dim, and damp;
Nor light, nor warmth, the rooms discover –
Bereft for years of fire and lamp.

The sun, sometimes in summer, enters
The casements, with reviving ray;
But the long rains of many winters
Moulder the very walls away.

And outside all is ivy, clinging
To chimney, lattice, gable grey;
Scarcely one little red rose springing
Through the green moss can force its way.

Unscared, the daw, and starling nestle,
Where the tall turret rises high.

And winds alone come near to rustle
The thick leaves where their cradles lie.

I sometimes think, when late at even
I climb the stair reluctantly,
Some shape that should be well in heaven,
Or ill elsewhere, will pass by me.

I fear to see the very faces,
Familiar thirty years ago,
Even in the old accustomed places
Which look so cold and gloomy now.

Further access strategies could be:

- ❦ Draw the house – use the illustration on page 104 to help you.
- ❦ Use the internet to research what relics might be found in the house. The poem was published as part of a collection in 1848.
- ❦ Read or listen to the whole poem to see which relics are mentioned: https://www.youtube.com/watch?v=JYlET-D_UYM.

Here is the passage that introduces these relics.

Resource 30

These fans of leaves, from Indian trees –
These crimson shells, from Indian seas –
These tiny portraits, set in rings –
Once, doubtless, deemed such precious things;

109

Keepsakes bestowed by Love on Faith,
And worn till the receiver's death,
Now stored with cameos, china, shells,
In this old closet's dusty cells.

Reading journeys

How many pupils can try a **hardest question first** approach?

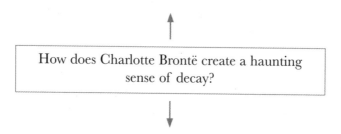

How does Charlotte Brontë create a haunting
sense of decay?

Support resources could be brief learning prompts:

- ❦ Find the words linked with anything overgrown.
- ❦ Is there a pattern to these images?
- ❦ How does the first-person narrator technique add to the atmosphere?
- ❦ How does the rhyme scheme contribute to the meaning?

❦ How does the layout in quatrains in the main extract support the flow and impact?

Bob says ...

*In this example, the prompts will act as success criteria. I use the phrase **learning prompts** so that detailed knowledge of literary devices can be introduced flexibly. If the pupils are told all the criteria, or given all the prompts, they may artificially regurgitate them but not understand them. By using the learning prompts according to need, you will be differentiating powerfully and including those with low ability in the reading journey. Only when gaps in knowledge materialise is it time to step in with a more formal session of explanation and modelling.*

Beyond the limit

For many of your pupils, you can expect **link reading** journeys to add significantly to their learning and participation. There is huge scope, including:

❦ The whole 'Mementos' poem: http://excellence-in-literature. com/poetry-2/mementos-by-charlotte-bronte.

❦ A burnt out Thornfield Hall in *Jane Eyre* by Charlotte Brontë (see Unit 14 of *Opening Doors to Famous Poetry and Prose*)

❦ The description of Miss Havisham in *Great Expectations* (see Unit 8 of *Opening Doors to Famous Poetry and Prose*)

❦ *The Graveyard Book* by Neil Gaiman

- *I Capture the Castle* by Dodie Smith
- *Shadowmancer* by G. P. Taylor

Wings to fly

The **routes to quality writing** diagram below gives options and possibilities for your young writers.

> Can you describe the rest of the outside of the house?

> 'The winds alone come near'. Write about someone or something else which also comes near to the overgrown house.

> Continue the story in poetry or prose.

> All in This House is Mossing Over

> Show how two or three of the relics found tell a story!

> Can you use images of nature (other than the ivy and red rose) to create a story or poem about decay?

> What else might the light through the casement window reveal?

They will have already learnt from the taster draft but further writing strategies could include:

🐛 Try planning the **denouement** (the finale) first.

🐛 Share ghostly settings with **talking partners** and leave each other with key questions on 'What next?' possibilities.

🐛 Sketch out three possible narratives before choosing the best one.

🐛 Try another taster draft to show how character and setting might develop together.

These strategies should support a whole-class discussion on what a really excellent ghostly atmosphere might be, so you might choose to mark the writing based on the conclusions. Just as the hardest question can come first, at least for some, consider the writing success criteria with the most ambitious expectation uppermost.

Excellent responses will:

🐛 Include an original expression of a decaying atmosphere.

🐛 Use punctuation creatively to add to the meaning.

🐛 Show a coherent link between character and setting.

Pupils who attended my Saturday Challenge enrichment centre worked with Charlotte Brontë's inspirational poem. I hope their literary creations will give you some further ideas about what might be possible.

The Winds Alone Come Near

The cruel winds whipped at the trees and the decaying house. Thick clouds rolled aimlessly in the sky. No sodden rain fell on the unkempt plot of land. Crinkled brown leaves fell from the frowning trees above. Sparrows and daws circled noisily overhead.

A few feet in front of me the dark winds rustled the heavy blanket of ivy. The crying wind spirits danced tauntingly in front of my eyes. I stood before the undiscovered wreck. No one knew what happened there years before. I imagined myself as a young girl with long, fair hair, unlike my ageing brown now, down to my waist, skipping merrily along the neatly cut lawns and laughing at the funny shapes the gardeners had made with the box hedges.

I stared longingly at the house before me. I remember that house in my visions, oh so clear. A new crimson, bricked cottage in the middle of a cosy sparse wood with a heavy oak door with blossoming honeysuckle round the door.

I was suddenly aware that the darkness and the deep wood were closing in …

Lara Bassett, Medstead School (Year 5)

All in This House is Mossing Over

In a dusty corner of the house of decay, a small box lay blanketed in cobwebs. It was made of ebony and covered in strange carvings; the letters of a foreign tongue. The lid was inlaid with mother-of-pearl and gold leaf, but the treasure locked inside was more valuable still.

Wrapped in slowly moulding silk was a jade elephant from the East. It had once hung from a necklace, sealed in a temple for centuries, high in the Himalayan Mountains. It had mystic powers, the locals said, made with magic for magic purposes. That was what made it so desirable. That was why the collector ripped it from the temple and brought it home. That day, the terror began.

Thomas Chan (Year 8)

Unit 10

Dancing the Skies

'High Flight' by John Gillespie Magee, Jr

Can you write poetry about very extreme and special emotions, about being in touch with something close to exhilaration?

Access strategies

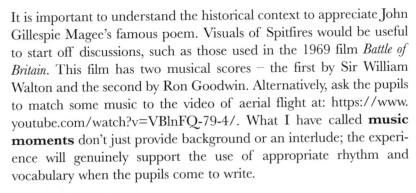

It is important to understand the historical context to appreciate John Gillespie Magee's famous poem. Visuals of Spitfires would be useful to start off discussions, such as those used in the 1969 film *Battle of Britain*. This film has two musical scores – the first by Sir William Walton and the second by Ron Goodwin. Alternatively, ask the pupils to match some music to the video of aerial flight at: https://www. youtube.com/watch?v=VBlnFQ-79-4/. What I have called **music moments** don't just provide background or an interlude; the experience will genuinely support the use of appropriate rhythm and vocabulary when the pupils come to write.

How much historical detail you wish to go into is down to you, but I would advise that you get the pupils to focus on the sheer exhilaration of flight:

❦ How often have you flown in an aeroplane?

❦ Have you ever experienced extreme speed?

❦ What does it feel like on a ride at a theme park?

❦ Who does not like that kind of experience and why?

Ask the children to compile a list of ten words or phrases they might use if they were writing about flying high in the sky. After five minutes, get them to share their words and decide as a group which ones are the best by placing sticky notes on a **continuum line** – the most appropriate words can go at one end with other suggestions ranged along the line. If flying is outside of their experience, ask them to use their imagination (and the stimulus of the video) to draft out some poetic phrases to sum up the potential beauty of flight. Each group must then give reasons for their choices of favourites. It will be a lively discussion!

The challenge now should be to write a **taster draft**, prose or poetry, to capture the beauty of flight in any kind of way – not necessarily in a Spitfire! Use **music moments** as opportunities for independence and investigation. Encourage your pupils to find classical pieces they like on the internet and write a draft about flight which matches the mood. If anyone is stuck, use 'Nimrod' from Elgar's *Enigma Variations*, the style of which will contrast with the scores for *Battle of Britain*.

It's now an option for you to read John Gillespie Magee's 'High Flight' to support the taster drafts. But you might feel your class is confident enough to experiment first and then deepen understanding by reading the poem afterwards.

High Flight

Oh! I have slipped the surly bonds of Earth
And danced the skies on laughter-silvered wings;
Sunward I've climbed, and joined the tumbling mirth
Of sun-split clouds, – and done a hundred things
You have not dreamed of – wheeled and soared and swung
High in the sunlit silence. Hov'ring there,
I've chased the shouting winds along, and flung
My eager craft through footless halls of air …

Up, up the long, delirious, burning blue
I've topped the wind-swept heights with easy grace.
Where never lark, or even eagle flew –
And, while with silent, lifting mind I've trod
The high untrespassed sanctity of space,
– Put out my hand and touched the face of God.

Reading journeys

Use the following evaluative question for the whole class and try to
choose the option box most appropriate for exploration. It could be
that the most able don't need support boxes but can analyse and
demonstrate comprehension without them – although they need to be

made aware of the richness of the imagery and clever technique in this poem.

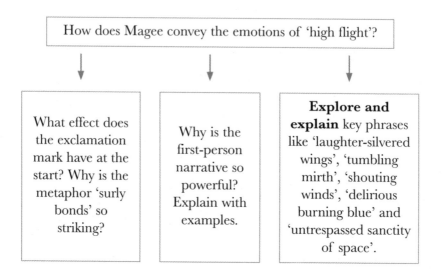

How does Magee convey the emotions of 'high flight'?

What effect does the exclamation mark have at the start? Why is the metaphor 'surly bonds' so striking?

Why is the first-person narrative so powerful? Explain with examples.

Explore and explain key phrases like 'laughter-silvered wings', 'tumbling mirth', 'shouting winds', 'delirious burning blue' and 'untrespassed sanctity of space'.

I think learning and reciting this poem can be very valuable. Practising the effects of the alliteration and the rhythms with an audience in mind can only enhance understanding. How many of your pupils can truly capture the absolute joy of speed and movement expressed by Magee?

Bob says ...

Some of the images in this poem are startlingly beautiful. I love the thinly veiled delight of Magee telling us that he's experienced 'what you have not dreamed of', and 'the sunlit silence' makes me imagine I am up there with him in the skies: a wonderful isolation! It's critical to relate the literary technique to the meaning being conveyed or the passion of a poem can be lost. Always share your favourite images with the class and ask for theirs too!

To **dig deeper**, relate the content to the sonnet form which Magee has used. You can find information about sonnets on many websites, including this one: http://www.sonnets.org/basicforms.htm.

The roots of the sonnet form lie in Italian poems about love and passion – *sonnetto* means 'little song' in Italian. Magee uses the sonnet form to build the ecstasy of flight for the first eight lines and then climb higher for the next six. Sometimes in sonnets a conflict in the feeling is introduced in the second section, but Magee adapts this into deepening the same argument – that he is leaving the limitations of earth behind and reaching out to God!

Sadly, Magee did not live long after writing this poem. He was serving in the Royal Canadian Air Force, based at RAF Digby in Lincolnshire, when his plane collided with another one during training in 1941. He was just 19 years old.

But the poem lives on. Just a few months before he died, he had enclosed 'High Flight' with a letter to his parents: 'I am enclosing a verse I wrote the other day. It started at 30,000 feet, and was finished soon after I landed. I thought it might interest you.'

You will find this website useful to find out more about how John's father passed the poem on and how it has had an extraordinary life of its own: http://www.highflightproductions.com. This includes:

❧ A recitation by Russell Crowe in the 1993 film *For the Moment.*

- An Orson Welles radio recording in 1946.

- A speech by US President Ronald Reagan after the Space Shuttle *Challenger* disaster.

- An appearance in *The Simpsons* – fame indeed!

- Its status as the official poem of the Royal Air Force and the Canadian Royal Air Force.

- In 1971, a copy was taken to the moon on *Apollo 15*.

- Don't miss Magee's mother reciting the poem!

The website was set up by Ray Haas who has also written a very impressive book called *Touching the Face of God* (2014). Haas has uncovered the story of the poet and the poem in extraordinary detail. Yes, an ordinary – and incredibly brave – person can jot down some memorable lines which can go on to inspire generations to come, but it also needs people like Ray Haas to be dedicated enough to tell the story!

You can find Magee's handwritten poem at: http://aviationpoetry. org/jgm_original_%20handwritten_poem.jpg.

Bob says ...

Great poetry can be written by very young people! You are passing on the legacy of this poem to the next generation. Why do I think it has endured? Well, I think, perhaps controversially, that it's not just about flying at all, but about any experience that reaches beyond the 'surly bonds of Earth' in any kind of way, the moments when we get closer to the indefinable – and it feels special!

Beyond the limit

The whole theme of the poem takes us beyond the limit. It is a superb context for creative thinking. Try deepening ideas with **link reading** of other sonnets:

- Shakespeare's sonnets, including number 18 ('Shall I compare thee to a summer's day?')
- 'How Do I Love Thee' by Elizabeth Barrett Browning
- 'The Mouse's Nest' by John Clare
- 'The Unreturning' by Wilfred Owen
- 'Ozymandias' by Percy Bysshe Shelley

Ask the pupils to research different types of sonnet. How does Magee adapt, for example, a Petrarchan sonnet?

Your pupils may enjoy parodies of 'High Flight'. There are a lot in *Slipping the Surly Bonds* by David English (1998). Titles include 'High Fright', 'Glider Flight' and 'Hog Flight' – and the writers of these poems often 'apologise' to Magee. Ray Haas is of the opinion that Magee would have loved every one of them! I've included parodying as an option in 'wings to fly'.

In addition, there is an opportunity for some pupils to compare 'High Flight' with 'An Irish Airman Foresees His Death' by W. B. Yeats. What similarities and differences in style and theme can they write about?

Some pupils might like to investigate further the idea of a poem becoming popular and enduring over many years. It would be a fascinating piece of detective work! It will be important for them to answer the question of why the poem has continued to be included in anthologies. It could be a poem for children or adults. To start the trail try:

❦ 'The Night Mail' by W. H. Auden

❦ The poetry of Emily Dickinson

❦ 'If –' by Rudyard Kipling

❦ 'Code Poem for the French Resistance' by Leo Marks

❦ Any nursery rhyme, such as 'Ring a Ring o' Roses'

Alternatively, ask the pupils to select a poem by a poet of today, perhaps by Simon Armitage, Grace Nicholls or Carol Ann Duffy. Why do they think it will endure?

Wings to fly

Never has this heading been so apt! The quality text has already done much to pave the way for quality writing. The following writing routes should now help:

❦ Decide on an area of interest connected with the theme of reaching to the stars (e.g. flight, space, beauty, freedom, art, a sporting triumph, an achievement). In other words, adapt the theme in a way which suits you. Use the stimulus of Magee's expression of joy to feed any appropriate idea.

❦ Focus on one or two of the striking images for inspiration. For example, 'laughter-silvered' and 'tumbling mirth' brilliantly link hilarity and joy with the actual plane. Could you include these techniques in your writing?

❦ Draft an ending first. Practise the possibility of changing tone at the end. 'High Flight' finishes with a spectacular assertion. How will you leave a strong impression on the reader?

❦ What kind of rhyme scheme will you use? Find out about different kinds of sonnet and use a rhyme scheme to complement your meaning.

❦ Practise some lines to experiment with tone. Do you think Magee is exhilarated? Is he 'delirious', to use his own word? What does that mean? Your poem should establish a consistent tone, although that mood can shift and change. Magee accelerates his delirium towards a crescendo ending.

❦ Will you use the first person?

I would suggest a good deal of flexibility and choice about whether the students use the sonnet form, but, if so, the 'love' written about can be an expression of joy just as in Magee's poem. It doesn't have to be a Shakespeare imitation along the lines of, 'Shall I compare thee to a summer's day?' but I'm sure you wouldn't want to stop anyone!

Complete drafts would be a good idea as the ideas develop. Then ask the pupils to discuss the drafts in groups and as a class. Ask your pupils to operate an **evidence circle** to find convincing reasons for choosing their favourite parts of the drafts. Peer group reading and evaluation can concentrate on where the poems are starting to be original. Ask the pupils to choose the poems they think show promise and then evidence that promise. You will want to give your own advice according to their progress.

The routes to writing will develop naturally into negotiated titles, but here are some more possibilities:

- Oh! I Have Slipped the Surly Bonds of Earth. Focus on a theme other than flight.

- Compose a sonnet entitled 'The Sunlit Silence'.

- You are the pilot of an eager craft but it could be in any time or space!

- Write about any exhilarating place that you feel privileged to inhabit.

- You are chasing the shouting winds where no lark or eagle flies. Where are you? Make the scene come alive for a reader.

- Can you adapt the sonnet form or follow a type of sonnet conventionally in order to parody 'High Flight'?

Excellent responses will:

- Apply some specific techniques learnt from Magee to some original poetry.

- Use a sonnet form effectively (if that is the format chosen).

- Use metaphors which are original and express the exhilaration of the moment.

I think you will be particularly inspired by Lucy's poem written in response to 'High Flight'. I hope her words will help your pupils to excel!

When the Sunset Falls

Amber wings burned against the falling sun's light.
As their wings flapped frantically, trying to escape the imminent darkness
The darkness which would kill,
Kill anything in its way …

It could hear the booming thunder from above,
And, as the air shook, a burst of light erupted from below.
But the sunset gave it hope,
The second best thing to freedom.

Its wings stopped as it took in the feeling of flight.
That wonderful feeling which fills you with joy.
That wonderful feeling which fills you with apprehension.
That wonderful feeling which fills you with dread.

Amber wings burned against the falling sun's light.
Burning with: joy, apprehension, dread and hope – enough to light up the darkness …

Lucy Harlow, Fort Hill Community School (Year 8)

The Mystery of the Lonely Merman

'The Forsaken Merman' by Matthew Arnold

How well can you adapt an inspiring poem to craft new forms and style?

Access strategies

Using the beginning and ending of Matthew Arnold's famous poem 'The Forsaken Merman' should stimulate some fantastic ideas on the mythology of mermaids and mermen. Try starting with some investigations on the definition of a merman. Exploring some examples from classical and modern traditions may help:

❧ Who was Triton?

❧ In which stories or films does he feature?

❧ What can you discover about merfolk from modern day comics, Disney films or Greek myths?

To practise the kind of thinking needed in the sustained writing later on, try asking the pupils to draft ideas for the middle section of this suggested story. Including more unusual possibilities in the planning stage can help to keep the focus on the imagination. Try simple **bookends** like these to promote quality thinking and risk-taking for story invention:

❦ Opening: Underwater setting featuring mermaid or merman

❦ Ending: Life underwater has changed forever!

If these openings and endings are the bookends, try to be very creative about the central section using this table:

Playing with possibilities	More unusual
Merman proves evil	Mythical sea creatures are responsible for the *Titanic* disaster!
Underwater world is threatened by mankind	
Merman rules Atlantis as a perfect place	

Now introduce your class to the beginning and the ending of 'The Forsaken Merman' and ask them to think about what may have happened to the children's mother. You may want to make the whole poem available at some point – it then becomes clear that the merman married a mortal human wife who has returned to her own community. You can find the whole poem here: http://www.poetryfoundation.org/poem/172845.

The Forsaken Merman (opening)

Come, dear children, let us away;
Down and away below.
Now my brothers call from the bay;
Now the great winds shorewards blow;
Now the salt tides seawards flow;
Now the wild white horses play,
Champ and chafe and toss in the spray.
Children dear, let us away!
This way, this way.

Call her once before you go.
Call once yet.
In a voice that she will know:
"Margaret! Margaret!"
Children's voices should be dear
(Call once more) to a mother's ear;
Children's voices, wild with pain.
Surely she will come again.
Call her once and come away.
This way, this way.
"Mother dear, we cannot stay!"
The wild white horses foam and fret.
Margaret! Margaret!

Come, dear children, come away down.
Call no more.
One last look at the white-wall'd town,
And the little grey church on the windy shore.
Then come down.
She will not come though you call all day.
Come away, come away.

(Final stanza)

But, children, at midnight,
When soft the winds blow;
When clear falls the moonlight;
When spring-tides are low:
When sweet airs come seaward
From heaths starr'd with broom;
And high rocks throw mildly
On the blanch'd sands a gloom
Up the still, glistening beaches,
Up the creeks we will hie;
Over banks of bright seaweed
The ebb-tide leaves dry.
We will gaze, from the sand-hills,
At the white, sleeping town;
At the church on the hill-side –
And then come back down.

Singing, "There dwells a lov'd one,
But cruel is she.
She left lonely for ever
The kings of the sea."

Reading journeys

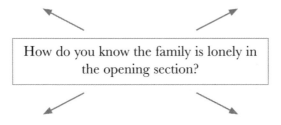

How do you know the family is lonely in
the opening section?

Excellent responses will include:

❦ Direct speech used for the calling of 'Margaret' acts as a desperate plea.

❦ Exclamation marks by the name suggest urgency and anxiety, a plea for Margaret to come.

❦ Repetition of 'calling' suggests that the family misses Margaret and wants her back.

❦ 'Wild with pain' is an extreme way of showing the children's agony.

❦ White horses (waves) are personified and the alliteration on the 'f' sound in 'foam and fret' emphasises an abrupt and anxious atmosphere. The waves call the family back under the sea but they have to return without their mother.

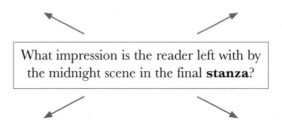

What impression is the reader left with by the midnight scene in the final **stanza**?

Excellent responses will include:

❦ Movement and rhythm grow through the rhyme scheme and the repetition of 'when'. An impression is given that they will always be out there waiting and watching.

❦ Exact settings like 'banks of bright seaweed' make the journey authentic and part of a routine.

❦ The punctuation supports the meaning: for example, the semi-colons divide the different images in the scene.

❦ The direct speech from the merman ends the poem with the emptiness of his loss.

There is plenty of **new learning** potential here and you may have to assess from the answers how much direct teaching you need to do to deepen your pupils' knowledge base. A **white space thinking** exercise in groups, highlighting key points and choosing favourite sections, would support confidence, growth and fun.

A **taster draft** here may help the pupils to prepare for the quality writing to come and give them a chance to practise new-found skills. Why not ask them to give more detail about one of the following in prose or poetry?

❦ The 'white, sleeping town'.

❦ The route the merman and his family take to slide up to the town.

❦ The underwater home of the merman.

For this last idea, perhaps read them Arnold's poem for inspiration. It describes the home of the merman:

Resource 35

> Sand-strewn caverns, cool and deep,
> Where the winds are all asleep;
> Where the spent lights quiver and gleam;
> Where the salt weed sways in the stream;
> Where the sea-beasts rang'd all round
> Feed in the ooze of their pasture-ground;
> Where the sea-snakes coil and twine,
> Dry their mail and bask in the brine;
> Where great whales come sailing by,
> Sail and sail, with unshut eye […]

Bob says ...

One of the difficult balances to find when teaching creative writing is to demonstrate techniques and open doors to challenging texts without smothering fresh imagination. Without the deeper knowledge and more explicit awareness, it's hard for understanding to grow; but with too much insistence on imitating an author or fulfilling teacher expectations, the outcomes can look all too similar. So, use what is learnt in the reading journeys to feed the imaginative possibilities in the minds of your young writers. Think 'wings to fly, not drills to kill'.

Beyond the limit

To go further than the investigations in the access strategies, try other poems and non-fiction accounts about mythical sea creatures:

❦ The Bishop Fish

❦ The Kelpie

❦ The Loch Ness Monster

❦ The Lorelei

❦ 'A Mermaid Song' by James Reeves

❦ 'The Kraken' and 'The Mermaid' by Alfred, Lord Tennyson

Of course, Hans Christian Andersen's *The Little Mermaid* is always popular – there is a good 2014 edition illustrated by Vilhelm Pedersen and Helen Stratton. The 1989 Disney film of *The Little Mermaid* will also prove useful.

For a further taster draft, why not ask pupils to imitate the idea of a community of sea creatures watching humanity from a hidden position, just like the merman's family? Ask them to imagine a family of krakens somewhere at night, watching but not wishing to be seen. Capturing that, like a still photograph in words, would be challenging but fascinating! A kraken is a mythical sea beast, often portrayed as squid-like. It is thought to be Nordic in origin but has tended to feature in all sorts of literature and films, sometimes connected with Greek myth.

Matthew Arnold is a famous poet and critic. You will find other poems by him at: http://famouspoetsandpoems.com/poets/matthew_ arnold/poems. 'The Forsaken Merman' was published in 1849 in *The Strayed Reveller*. Arnold also worked as one of Her Majesty's Inspectors of Schools and is therefore in a direct line to the HMIs who lead Ofsted inspections today!

Wings to fly

Now is a good time to ask for recitals of parts of the poem. Emphasise the way the rhythm helps us to understand the cycles of the merman's visits to the town and the emptiness he finds. Spelling work on words like 'though', 'glistening' and 'midnight' should be helpful here. As your pupils have to read the words aloud, your advice is more likely to be heeded – and they will be able to visualise the 'ght' of 'night' and the 'e' in 'glistening'. The recitation should help them to enjoy the poem, so now is a good time to move to the quality writing stage.

Potential titles could revolve around key questions raised by the reading journey:

❦ Why did Margaret return to her human home?

❦ Could there have been a different ending?

❦ How do beginnings and endings lend shape to a narrative poem?

❦ What kind of underwater society is hinted at? Can this be developed?

Use the following **radial questions** diagram to negotiate the right title for each pupil. Any of the titles could be completed as poetry or prose. Extend the thinking from the access strategies stage because this will reaffirm the importance of unusual plot lines and stretching the imagination.

Bob says ...

Quality texts require deeper reading journeys - but that means original thinking becomes more of a habit. Routines are vital in a learning environment, so try to plan the transfer of new understanding from the extract into bold and quirky creative writing to complete the unit.

She Will Not Come Though You Call All Day

You must explain in a central section why the merman's human wife had to return home. Is it as cruel as it sounds?

Up the Still Glistening Beaches

Show the merman's family using a different part of the beach to creep near the town. How will you make it dramatic?

Ideas for using the beginning and ending (the bookends) of 'The Forsaken Merman' for inspired writing

The White, Sleeping Town

In your central section, describe more of the town and include an apparent sighting of the merman by humans.

Come Away, Come Away

Write a central section – remembering to build the tension – and invent a suitable alternative ending.

Margaret! Margaret!

The idea of a mortal woman becoming part of an undersea family is total fantasy. How can you make your reader believe it actually happened? Write the story of the merman's human wife, Margaret, as the central section, with a different ending if you need it.

For all the writing titles, **excellent responses will**:

❦ Use a rhythm which gives the sense of an epic story, rising in pitch towards the end.

❦ Develop tension, just as in Arnold's poem.

❦ Build a sense of drama, captured through the atmosphere and key events.

❦ Link the central section with the bookends.

Unit 12

Making Magic Talk

'The Magnifying Glass'
by Walter de la Mare

How well can you experiment with fresh images and still make the final writing coherent and complete?

Access strategies

You can use the wonderfully imaginative 'The Magnifying Glass' by Walter de la Mare to show your pupils how image making can be great fun and a planning tool for coherent creative writing.

Start with these images from the poem:

Resource 36

With this round glass
I can make *Magic* talk –
A myriad shells show
In a scrap of chalk;

Of but an inch of moss
A forest – flowers and trees;
A drop of water
Like a hive of bees.

A **noticed/noted/not sure** chart can help with the exploration of all the images in these opening **stanzas**.

Noticed	Noted	Not sure
Are shells in chalk?	Looks like chalk is partly micro-fossils.	I need to find out about 'myriad'. I think he is saying there are lots of shells that we could see with the help of a microscope.
Inch of moss		
Drop of water like a hive		
Why is 'Magic' in italics?		

Bob says ...

*Simple **thinking engines** like this one can turn the exercise into a genuine investigation and emphasise independent thinking. Your pupils can stretch themselves in terms of knowledge acquisition as well as learning capacity (using the internet if available). Keep prompting them with more questions and directions for learning if they get stuck.*

Now, consider that this poem was written in 1941. Using a magnifying glass would have seemed a lot of fun in an age decades before computers and the sophisticated technology which with we are now familiar. Try listing the many different ways in which we now expand a view, blow up a scene or get a closer look at something that is a long way away. There might be some quite unusual examples to be found in the worlds of medicine or science which will be new to many of the pupils. Think about examples in the classroom too, like visualisers.

Ask groups of pupils to gather images inspired by any modern way of zooming in or expanding our normal view. Possible subjects might be:

❦ A close-up of a planet.

❦ The palm of a hand.

❦ A hugely magnified view of a plant.

❦ Inside a mobile phone.

❦ A follicle of hair.

Encourage them to come up with lots of possibilities and then select the top five per group. The criteria should be based around the potential for creative writing. After discussion and tips, ask them to produce a **taster draft** of an opening paragraph or **stanza** of a very imaginative piece. It's a chance for them to experiment with images and word power! The most successful drafts will imitate de la Mare's sense of wonder.

Those writers who use a first-person narrator may like to convey that sense of magic in seeing the world in a different way. Of course, de la Mare (with his magnifying glass) has a great sense of control over what he sees and where he moves the glass – 'I can make *Magic* talk', he says – so your pupils might like to think about this too.

There should be potential here for some philosophical thinking:

🐛 How important is it to reflect upon the wonder of the world?

🐛 If something is magnified do we understand it differently?

🐛 Are you in control of your world?

Bob says ...

*Sapere is the Society for the Advancement of Philosophical Enquiry and Reflection in Education and promotes **Philosophy for Children**: http://www.sapere.org.uk. I have seen the huge benefits to children of receiving integrated thinking, debating and questioning skills via P4C. It's not a discrete activity – philosophical thinking at stages like this will significantly deepen reading and writing skills. The resulting engagement is often memorable and helps to make poetry fun too!*

After a **mini-plenary** with explorations and advice about effective drafts or problems, the full poem will be heard with absorbed interest. What other images does de la Mare use?

Resource 38

The Magnifying Glass

With this round glass
I can make *Magic* talk –
A myriad shells show

In a scrap of chalk;

Of but an inch of moss
A forest – flowers and trees;
A drop of water
Like a hive of bees.

I lie in wait and watch
How the deft spider jets
The woven web-silk
From his spinnerets;

What tigerish claws he has!
And oh! the silly flies
That stumble into his snare –
With all those eyes!

Not even the tiniest thing
But this my magic glass
Will make more marvellous,
And itself surpass.

Yes, and with lenses like it,
Eyeing the moon,
'Twould seem you'd walk there
In an afternoon!

Reading journeys

Focus on the kinds of comprehension skills that will help your pupils to make the bridge between how de la Mare builds wonder and how a modern piece of writing could update some of the same feelings.

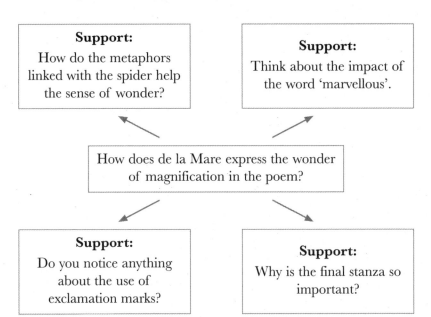

Support:
How do the metaphors linked with the spider help the sense of wonder?

Support:
Think about the impact of the word 'marvellous'.

How does de la Mare express the wonder of magnification in the poem?

Support:
Do you notice anything about the use of exclamation marks?

Support:
Why is the final stanza so important?

Bob says ...

The 'Opening Doors' strategies always pitch high in terms of open questions which encourage an evaluation of the whole text. Differentiation via varied learning opportunities and interventions can then follow.

Beyond the limit

Link reading could focus on Walter de la Mare as a poet. He has written many creative and accessible poems, often about nature, emotions and wonder. 'The Listeners' has been a favourite in classrooms for a long time but you could also suggest:

- 'A Robin'
- 'All That's Past'
- 'Arabia'
- 'Nicholas Nye'
- 'Silver'

Another link into **wider reading** would be poems focusing on the awe of new, imaginative possibilities. These suggestions include a variety of styles:

- 'Total Solar Eclipse' by Valerie Bloom
- 'Amulet' by Ted Hughes
- 'Unending Sky' by John Masefield
- Chinese poems in *The Penguin Book of Chinese Verse*

Potential anthologies for your pupils to devise could centre around images of wonder and new striking ways of seeing the world!

Wings to fly

The earlier taster drafts can now become very exciting sustained pieces in poetry or prose. Some of the deeper learning will already have been accomplished. The following titles and ideas are more like prompts to support possible writing routes as your writers will already have learnt a lot about their preferred images and the importance of originality.

- 'Twould seem you'd walk there in an afternoon' says de la Mare. What other images could you include in your writing, other than ones connected with the moon? Combine them into sustained writing which is original.

- 'With this _____ I can make magic talk'. Rather than a magnifying glass, what object will you use which creates the zoom effect?

- Write a close-up version of one or two of the following:
  - Beans
  - A finger nail
  - A car radio
  - A bird's nest
  - An eye
  - Your choice!

These will need researching but that's part of the challenge! Your pupils should be encouraged to understand high expectations in terms of the following **excellent responses will** list:

- Create original images.

- Use images in a coherent way in prose or poetry.

❦ Craft a flowing piece of writing using connective strategies to avoid the impression of a list.

❦ Use writing strategies, like figures of speech, for striking effect.

❦ Use punctuation to enhance the reading and meaning.

I think the magnification idea has huge scope for very original work if risks are taken and your pupils work hard enough to improve and adapt their image making on the writing journey. Celebrate the outcomes but also include signposting where necessary because challenging writing like this should ensure **new learning**. Even the most able need to encounter fresh struggles.

Unit 13

The Spirit in the Garden

'A Garden at Night' by James Reeves

Can you respond to the challenge of writing an original night scene?

Access strategies

Before exploring 'A Garden at Night' by James Reeves, list the descriptions of plants and nature in the poem and ask your pupils to find pictures on the internet which might represent them:

- Petals
- Grass
- Poppy
- Lavender
- Roses
- Fruit
- Orchard
- Garden

Can they use some of these images in a description of their own about a garden by day? It could be in poetry or prose. Extravagant examples from the Chelsea Flower Show or Hampton Court Palace Flower

Show might stretch the imagination into the area of garden design. Offer maximum choice on writing about a larger, older garden or a smaller, more modern one. Their garden should have a particular feel or atmosphere of its own. For excellent responses, emphasise that the plants should have a distinctive quality or aura. Including the people who use the garden may help the process. Does the gardener fit the garden?

Now ask the pupils how the garden scene would look different at night. They should craft and compose a single **stanza** or paragraph first with a focus on the poppy.

❦ How will the poppy's leaves look different?

❦ Can you imagine a night creature in the garden near the poppy?

❦ Is it a moonlit night?

❦ Is it cold?

❦ Does the flower bed around the poppy seem different?

❦ Are you writing your piece from any particular perspective?

These **taster drafts** should produce words, phrases and images which you can help them to refine into original ideas about the day/night contrast. For those pupils finding it tough to respond to the poppy, emphasise more the night atmosphere, the noises and the creatures who could be roaming, as this may hook them more.

Take the chance to improve spelling, punctuation and grammar. When your pupils are proud of their drafts and you are advising on style, why not integrate a session on spelling rules, word derivation or suffixes? In context, there can be even more engagement with the ways in which spelling, punctuation and grammar contribute to meaning. If a pupil has misspelt 'definite' as 'definate' in a draft, there can be no better time to launch into some advice on the structures of words and sounds. By dividing the 'de' from 'finite', it becomes easier to remember that it has got two 'i's. Then 'finite' can be explained as a word in itself. It is likely to be a combination of memorisation and understanding that fixes a spelling securely in the mind but, as with all learning, the learner must be engaged. At the point of writing, more pupils are likely to be curious than in separate spelling, punctuation and grammar sessions.

Now ask your pupils to compare their draft with James Reeves's poem. Watch the look on their faces as you read 'A Garden at Night'. Pictures of spooky garden scenes could be on a PowerPoint loop with appropriate music as an accompaniment – try *Nights in the Gardens of Spain* by Manuel de Falla which he completed in 1915. It's for piano and orchestra and has three parts or movements, each one evoking a different garden.

A Garden at Night

Resource 39

On powdery wings the white moths pass,
And petals fall on the dewy grass;
Over the bed where the poppy sleeps
The furtive fragrance of lavender creeps.
Here lived an old lady in days long gone,
And the ghost of that lady lingers on.
She sniffs the roses, and seems to see
The ripening fruit on the orchard tree;

Like the scent of flowers her spirit weaves
Its winding way through the maze of leaves;
Up and down like the moths it goes:
Never and never it finds repose.
Gentle she was, and quiet and kind,
But flitting and restless was her old mind.
So hither and thither across the lawn
Her spirit wanders, till grey of dawn
Rouses the cock in the valley far,
And the garden waits for the morning star.

Reading journeys

'Never and never it finds repose' is a key line. The repetition is like a final underlining that the old lady will wander restlessly until the end of time. Insist that your pupils find every possible image or inferred suggestion that her spirit is wandering. One way is to use an **evidence spotlight** approach where pupils, in groups, select their favourite three images and debate their choices with reasons. Use ICT to highlight or display potential evidence choices and make the case for the way Reeves matches structure and rhyme to his theme. Here is an example:

Spotlight on ...	Reasons	Questions
Like the scent of flowers her spirit weaves its winding way	The simile makes me think of a pleasant scent. It's comforting. The old lady does not move in a straight line but winds through the garden like the scent.	She seems happy. Yet she never finds rest, so is this good or bad?

Bob says ...

You will have to intervene accordingly as the debates across the groups or class take place. This is the best time to teach new knowledge about poetry – at the point of engagement and interest, not as a discrete section of learning.

You should be looking for some of these **excellent responses** and can prompt pupils as appropriate:

- Words and phrases like 'maze of leaves' and 'winding way' suggest a rambling garden and a restless ghost – there is a relationship between the two.

- The **rhyming couplets** are not just pleasant on the ear – they emphasise the gentle meanderings of the old lady.

- The full stop after 'repose' which is linked with the repetition of 'never' leaves a sense of pain. Is she doomed to wander forever without rest? Or is the garden where she belongs?

- An explanation of how vocabulary like 'hither and thither' and 'flitting and restless' support the perpetual motion of the lady.

- The single stanza layout beautifully supports the coherence of the night-time visitation as it helps us to imagine the spirit moving seamlessly through her garden.

Beyond the limit

Dig deeper for the more able with key questions after they read Berlie Doherty's 'Ghost in the Garden': http://www.poetryarchive. org/poem/ghost-garden.

❧ In what ways is this poem both similar to and different from James Reeves's 'A Garden at Night'?

❧ Which poem do you prefer and why?

It would be apt to read *The Secret Garden* by Frances Hodgson Burnett to link with this unit as it's probably the most famous children's story with a garden setting and has plenty of mystery too. (It features in Unit 12 of *Opening Doors to Quality Writing for Ages 6–9*.)

'Haunted Houses' by Henry Wadsworth Longfellow may not be about a garden but it does explore the idea that we may leave a mark, a shadow, a presence on our surroundings: https://www.poets.org/ poetsorg/poem/haunted-houses.

There are many poems by Thomas Hardy which could be included in **link reading** on the theme of personalities leaving some kind of trace on their surroundings and environment – for example:

❧ 'Old Furniture' (see Unit 17 of *Opening Doors to Famous Poetry and Prose*)

❧ 'The Haunter'

❧ 'Voices from Things Growing in a Churchyard'

❧ 'Where the Picnic Was'

For more quality writing, why not keep to the night scene objective but ask the pupils to apply it to a setting other than a garden? It is the capturing of the night sounds, the chill and the wakefulness of the senses that will help your young writers to stretch themselves beyond the limit!

Wings to fly

If the reading journeys have been rigorous, this will feed into the ambition of the creative writing. Try a writing process where pupils can now choose a broad area to explore and begin to find their own title. Think of it as posing **quality options** for your pupils. They must choose a challenging route inspired by the poem but may have to develop ideas on all routes before deciding which one to pursue. The exercise should encourage reflection and negotiation as well as independence.

Here are some potential areas:

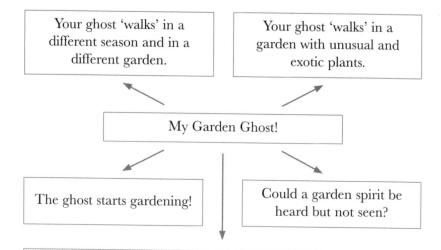

Your ghost 'walks' in a different season and in a different garden.

Your ghost 'walks' in a garden with unusual and exotic plants.

My Garden Ghost!

The ghost starts gardening!

Could a garden spirit be heard but not seen?

Insert more lines into the same poem after 'repose'. Develop images of the moon, the greenhouse and the pond.

Bob says ...

Processes like the quality options reflections should lead your pupils into more thinking about which kinds of titles or routes actually offer creative scope. They will start to realise for themselves that their best work is more likely to emerge from ambition and risk-taking rather than a tried and trusted conventional title. The poet Sylvia Plath said, 'everything in life is writable about if you have the outgoing guts to do it, and the imagination to improvise. The worst enemy to creativity is self-doubt.'

Unit 14

A Shropshire Lad

'Blue Remembered Hills'
by A. E. Housman

Can you explore the elusiveness of memory and turn your ideas into some memorable writing?

Access strategies

Before any exposure to the poem, ask your pupils to list five memories from when they were very young which could be positive or negative. It might be a memory about a person, place, accident or unexpected happening. Get them to share these with each other in **evidence circles** – the reasons given for choosing each memory should be striking. To encourage listening, insist that you will ask for feedback on the most interesting memories heard. If the best ones are written up on an interactive whiteboard, additional impressions can be added by the individuals whose memories have been chosen.

Next, try these questions as a whole-class discussion:

❦ Are our memories reliable?

❦ Have you remembered the incident or feeling accurately?

❦ Does what happened seem different in any way as you now recollect it?

A **taster draft** should convert the thinking energy into written outcomes. Ask for a piece of writing which recreates the atmosphere – rather than recounts the events – of a day long ago when your pupils were very young. Suggest that **excellent responses will** emphasise sounds, impressions and perhaps a key emotion. Your **mini-plenary** can include advice on making an impact with images and being original. Try including in any mini-plenary a question around difficulties:

❦ What have you struggled with?

❦ What did you get stuck on?

This can help you to give advice where it's needed before unpicking the successes which can be shared and celebrated.

Bob says ...

If you search online for images of 'blue remembered hills' you will find stills from Dennis Potter's 1979 play of the same name, as well as actual blue mountains. Potter cleverly used adult actors dressed as children which emphasised the profound complexity of how we remember the past. A mountain can look blue when seen from a distance, so this can help your pupils to understand the image and what it might mean or symbolise. But what colour is it really? Get them to think about how light and shade can change the way we see mountain slopes, even over just a few minutes.

You can now use the **key image** of blue mountains to access some complex ideas. Put the blue mountain images on a PowerPoint loop and ask your pupils to examine the illustration on page 164 simultaneously. Ask them the following questions:

❦ What can mountains symbolise in the imagination?

❦ Do you have any associations with blue mountains?

You are now going to share with them a brief but famous poem. What angle on memories might it have? Try using sticky notes around the illustration to develop possible ideas that link memories with blue mountains.

A. E. Housman wrote sixty-three poems which make up *A Shropshire Lad*, which was published in 1896. The poems are about an idealised country world, perhaps an attempt to return to the ideal of the pastoral idyll which had been popular in the previous century. This is poem number 40 and is one of the most well-known, possibly because it makes everyone wonder about the bittersweet nature of fond memories.

Resource 41

Into my heart an air that kills
　　From yon far country blows:
What are those blue remembered hills,
　　What spires, what farms are those?

That is the land of lost content,
　　I see it shining plain,

The happy highways where I went
And cannot come again.

Reading journeys

The second key image which merits exploration is the first line, 'Into
my heart an air that kills':

❦ What associations are there with the word 'heart'?

❦ What does 'an air that kills' mean?

If any of the pupils are stuck, try a visual mapping approach which tracks the air on its journey. Where I have added words, ask your pupils to find or draw images. This might take them closer to understanding how a memory, although experienced as enjoyable at the time, becomes 'lost content' when it fades.

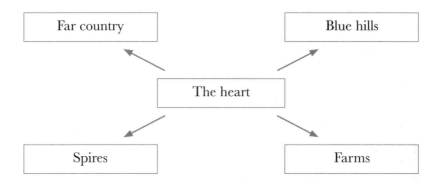

This seems the right time to commit the poem to memory and ask pupils to recite it, with the aim of deepening their understanding. Some might like to make a film with accompanying music and turn their rendering into something very moving, perhaps with rural scenes and mountains. A PowerPoint slide show, timed to move on appropriately as they speak the words, is another practical suggestion. It needs to be great fun; if so, the sounds and rhythms should take root.

The poet Roger McGough says in an article in *Teach Reading and Writing* (2015) that many of his friends can 'remember those rhythms, rhymes and metaphors; your head may forget a poem, but if it has touched you, your heart will retain and thrill to it'. Roger is careful to remind us, though, that just learning poems for the sake of it is much less valuable.

Beyond the limit

Try recommending that the pupils research writers who have been fascinated by memories from the past, but they should remember that the theme is the complexity of how we view reminiscences. The following may help:

❦ 'It Was Long Ago' by Eleanor Farjeon

❦ 'I Remember, I Remember' by Thomas Hood

❦ 'A Visit to Grandpa's' by Dylan Thomas

❦ *Grandad with Snails* by James Baldwin

❦ *Boy: Tales of Childhood* by Roald Dahl

❦ *Cider with Rosie* by Laurie Lee

Your pupils will have varied views on how we remember the past and this could be exploited in an anthology, perhaps called 'Moving Memories'. Here is a chance for them to become the next Housman or Lee!

Wings to fly

Before launching into the extended writing, it is worth enforcing the lessons that have been learnt from the reading journey:

❦ Can you imitate the murderous quality of the metaphorical use of 'air'?

❦ Can you invent and use convincingly a metaphor that reverses our usual expectations. After all, air normally keeps us alive! It's used as a **paradox**.

❦ Can you use key images in your writing, especially in poetry, which hit the senses with an **ambiguity** of meaning?

❦ Can you develop your own view of memory and the past (which is likely to be very different from Housman's)?

This can form the basis of your **excellent responses will** criteria and sets up much more ambitious writing than is sometimes the case. Before considering the titles and ideas below, here are a few more suggestions to assist with the writing process:

❦ Why edit? Why draft? I always emphasise that the children write taster drafts early on in the process to capture the joy of being stimulated by a discussion, a poem or an inspired session of teaching. Some drafts I come across in schools are long and repetitive, often showing little improvement and sometimes accompanied by a request: 'Is it time to copy up now?' Somewhere in the middle of all of this the spontaneity of writing can be lost.

But there is another side to it too. I have also encountered very able writers who dash out a few promising lines but then seem to lose interest, feeling that the job is done. It might be worth demonstrating the value of editing by referring to the changes A. E. Housman made to his poem. According to the Housman Association, he originally considered 'dissolving hills' or 'faint bewildering hills'. Try a **plus, minus, interesting** chart to debate the difference and learn how much it matters!

Plus	Minus	Interesting
Blue remembered hills		
Dissolving hills		
Faint bewildering hills		

❦ Does **metre** matter? The poem is written in lines alternating eight and six syllables. If your pupils recited it well, then they may understand more about the kind of rhythm it offers – the longer lines with the regular **iambic** beat have a resonance which the rhyme scheme further enforces. If your pupils understand how the line, 'What are those blue remembered hills', is structured – and therefore spoken – they can start to imitate and adapt such conventions.

The best writing is likely to come from fulfilling the original objective of taking a fresh look at memories. Here are some possible routes:

❦ Take an image other than hills but make it the centre of your poem or story. It must reflect a way of interpreting memory.

❦ Focus on a 'first time' memory. It might be the first day at school or first time abroad. Can you remember the first time you were allowed to go out by yourself? What about your first friend?

❦ Write a poem or story based around a strongly felt emotion that is still in the memory. Can you create the haze of the past in your use of language?

❦ Focus on a method for looking at a memory in an original way. Are you 'seeing' it through a kind of prism? Plan the method first, then match this to the content.

Or try a focused approach based on remembering:

❦ My Old Home

❦ A Christmas Day

❦ The Holiday Nightmare

❦ Fear

❦ Laughter at Infants School

❦ First Teacher

❦ Discovering the World Beyond Home

❦ My Sister or Brother's Arrival

❦ Moving House

❦ The Disaster!

There is no hierarchy in these routes. Why not invent more and distribute them according to ability or let the pupils choose their writing route? You are looking for fresh crafting of ideas, not a standard narrative or poem. Housman's 'blue remembered hills' can seem a little bleak, but your pupils can use what they learn from the techniques to forge their own inspired writing.

Bob says ...

Reading Housman's verse made me think about how I remember my past. I hope you will find my story 'Ice Paths' (see Appendix) enjoyable to read. It is based more on the way I remember the atmosphere of growing up in 1963 than a recreation of any one event; but the free, roaming childhood and the friends I knew will always swim in the imagination. Have I proved Housman wrong by revisiting my 'happy highways'? Why not write up your own memories and share your script with your pupils and, I hope, with me?

Unit 15

The Silver Heel

'I Started Early – Took My Dog' by Emily Dickinson

How well can you write about the same subject in different styles?

Access strategies

Imagine a scene long ago – a woman walking her dog by the sea. There is a town adjacent to the sea and there are warships (frigates) visible on the horizon. The tide starts to come in.

❧ What might the woman be thinking about?

❧ What kind of poetry might be possible?

❧ What mood is suggested by the illustration on page 174?

It's always a good idea to call on your pupils' own experiences. Focus on the tide and ask them to think of any day when they visited the coast and saw the tide a long way out or very much moving in. What do they remember about it? How did the coastal landscape change as the tide came in?

Breathe life into the scene by asking for a **taster draft** from the point of view of the tide. It's what I call a **javelin** task – thrown high, moving fast and making an impact! Your pupils need to use **personification** in any kind of poetry or prose, giving the tide its own feelings. It could be a male or female tide! Ask them to create an imaginative scene – they can even include the dog!

For further support, use the example of the famous causeway across to St Michael's Mount in Cornwall and ask the pupils to imagine the viewpoint of the tide if it were given emotions of its own. Lihou Island on Guernsey is another good example of where tides are constantly changing the landscape.

Like all quality writing, it is finding originality that is the greatest challenge. So why not put the **evidence spotlight** on unusual ideas which seem to be coherent? Of course, it's not just about long words or overused similes but more about the right word in the right place. In Emily Dickinson's poem, she uses the image of a 'Silver heel' to personify the pursuing tide. It's a beautiful and vivid phrase which says just enough. Train your pupils to select and evaluate writing potential in the work of their peers too, not just their own.

Bob says ...

I try to ensure that pupils at my writing workshops engage with one another – not just for fun, but to learn how to identify creative potential in their friends' work. I ask them to comment on their peers' progress in order to keep them learning from others too. It can help to shape a community of young writers and make the process popular across the class.

Reading journeys

You will have dipped into this book in random order, I'm sure, but as this is the last unit I thought I would signpost the way forward with your own resourcing by including:

❧ Just a light touch suggestion of where the language learning might be at its deepest.

❧ A chance for your pupils to show they can understand the effects of different styles under a similar theme.

Linking the extracts and poems with other texts has been a constant theme throughout this book under the 'beyond the limit' heading; indeed, it is the main route to long-term progress. But I think it would be a challenge for your pupils to be given a more open opportunity to see how well they can identify styles and intention and then use the inspiration in their own quality writing. This will provide the kind of practice needed to prepare for work on 'unseen' poetry and prose when no teacher support is possible.

How much analysis can they do themselves if you now show them the Emily Dickinson poem?

Resource 43

I Started Early – Took My Dog

I started Early – Took my Dog –
And visited the Sea –
The Mermaids in the Basement

Came out to look at me –

And Frigates – in the Upper Floor
Extended Hempen Hands –
Presuming Me to be a Mouse –
Aground – upon the Sands –

But no Man moved Me – till the Tide
Went past my simple Shoe –
And past my Apron – and my Belt
And past my Bodice – too –

And made as He would eat me up –
As wholly as a Dew
Upon a Dandelion's Sleeve –
And then – I started – too –

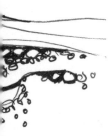

And He – He followed – close behind –
I felt His Silver Heel
Upon my Ankle – Then my Shoes
Would overflow with Pearl –

Until We met the Solid Town –
No One He seemed to know –
And bowing – with a Mighty look –
At me – The Sea withdrew –

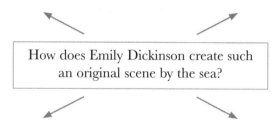

How does Emily Dickinson create such
an original scene by the sea?

Try to encourage **white space thinking** as much as possible.
Talking partners can work through possible answers, and sticky
notes have their perennial place around the edges if you use large
sheets of sugar paper. Why not use different colour sticky notes for
answers and the evidence to support them?

Use the following prompts for any pupils who are stuck:

❦ What is the effect of the frequent use of capital letters?

❦ Why are there so many dashes and how does that influence the
meaning?

❦ Can you show the cumulative effect of the clever but simply
expressed figures of speech – for example, 'Dew upon a
Dandelion's Sleeve', 'overflow with Pearl' or 'Solid Town'?

❦ How does the rhythm and rhyme scheme contribute to the
meaning?

❦ How do you know the poem was written a long time ago?

❦ Could the poem be about broader themes, or is the tide a
metaphor?

If the access strategies have been successful your pupils should start to get absorbed in the process of appreciating the poem. There is so much to say! That is the sign of a quality text – one which engages but also needs lots of reflection.

Now, ask them to compare Dickinson's poem with a very different one by Henry Wadsworth Longfellow.

Resource 45

The Tide Rises, the Tide Falls

The tide rises, the tide falls,
The twilight darkens, the curlew calls;
Along the sea-sands damp and brown
The traveller hastens toward the town,
And the tide rises, the tide falls.

Darkness settles on roofs and walls,
But the sea in the darkness calls and calls;
The little waves, with their soft white hands,
Efface the footprints in the sands,
And the tide rises, the tide falls.

The morning breaks; the steeds in their stalls
Stamp and neigh, as the hostler calls;
The day returns, but nevermore
Returns the traveller to the shore,
And the tide rises, the tide falls.

Now see if your pupils can take the chart below much further by thinking deeply about style and meaning in the two poems.

Poem	Meaning	Style	Comments and links
I Started Early – Took my Dog	All about the walker's relationship with the tide. It threatens her but she resists its power.	Figures of speech used to reflect her feelings. She sees the tide as a person, a masculine presence.	
The Tide Rises, the Tide Falls	A dedication. Nature is eternal.	Repetition adds a musical structure.	Interesting link as both poems include **personifica-tion**.

Encourage the pupils to use the comments and links column as a very open-ended opportunity to ask questions, note fresh ideas and draw comparisons. Cross-referencing may be more challenging but it's also going to add significantly to your pupils' repertoire as budding writers. Comparing and contrasting texts sits very naturally with the 'beyond the limit' stretch and challenge ethos promoted in 'Opening Doors'. The **link reading**, the philosophy, the thinking skills and the deeper learning all contribute to quality writing. Samuel Johnson, deviser of the English dictionary, said: 'The greatest part of a writer's time is spent in reading, in order to write; a man will turn over half a library to make one book.'

Beyond the limit

The comparison of styles can be deepened by including some of the texts below. There is nothing wrong with comparing poetry with prose, but it's important to remember that particular genres and styles are always selected for a reason and that the style should match the subject. This will be the major learning point for your pupils when they come to write.

Poems about the sea which might provide further variety include:

- 'The Forsaken Merman' by Matthew Arnold (see Unit 11)
- 'The Mermaid's Purse' by Ted Hughes in *Collected Poems for Children*
- 'Sea Fever' by John Masefield
- 'The Sea' by James Reeves
- 'Slowly' by James Reeves (see Unit 3 in *Opening Doors to Quality Writing for Ages 6–9*)

Poems by Emily Dickinson:

- 'Hope'
- 'The Sea of Sunset'
- 'Snake' (see Unit 6 of *Opening Doors to Famous Poetry and Prose*)
- 'A Thunderstorm'

Emily Dickinson has become one of America's greatest poets, yet she spent much of her life on the family homestead and it was her sister who got her work published after she had died. Her work is very original and yet can seem effortless – and that is challenging to imitate!

Wings to fly

This unit has given your pupils an opportunity to explore contrasting styles and become more independent in doing so. Now they can experiment further with a range of possibilities inspired by the ocean theme.

Ask the pupils to choose two of the following titles and ideas about the tide for a poem of their own, and to ensure that they are written so that form and technique match the subject:

❦ Tidal Power

❦ Low Tide at Dawn

❦ Stranded!

❦ The Rock Pool

❦ The Truth About What Happened to Emily Dickinson's Dog!

❦ My Silver Heel

❦ How My Beach World and the Tide Met Face To Face!

❦ The Tide and the Moon

❦ 'There is a tide in the affairs of men' (*Julius Caesar* by William Shakespeare). Write a poem using the tide metaphorically.

❦ King Canute's Strategy! A rewriting of a famous tale.

And/or make the **personification** of the sea and/or the tide central to a longer narrative poem which might have as its theme:

- Childhood
- Fear
- Power
- Beauty
- Nature

These are huge possibilities with which to end *Opening Doors to Quality Writing*, but let's not call it an ending. The doors to some of the biggest themes to inspire and perplex writers down the years have been opened by your energetic and imaginative teaching. Let your students go through the doors. In the words of the poet Brian Moses (in an interview for the English Association): 'If you want to be a writer, write! Don't just talk about doing it, do it.'

'Ice Paths: A Fetcham Tale' by Bob Cox

The fog lifted but the ice remained. It was always winter, even after Christmas. In the night I breathed a smoky world before me and shivered down to the toilet. One night I crept softly back upstairs but tripped by my sister's doll's house. Crisp frost spread like spiders' webs across the window but a fierce moon cast a ray through the ice onto the garden of the doll's house. A single small figure pushed a lawn mower over the green felt. I moved lots of figures out of the rooms and onto the lawn as the silver ray slid across the world of the dolls.

But spring did not come anywhere else. At school we were banned from sliding down the top playground but did so anyway until Miss Rivers arrived with a salt bag and threats. The lollipop man was a living snowman for us. He wore white, he looked white and he was called Mr White! With his help, we cleared a path to school and lessons continued through the winter. The boilers broke down and we worked on, wearing huge coats and bobble hats. Then the boilers worked too well and we stripped down to vests like it was summer! Every morning, the caretaker shovelled in more coal, his wellington boots cracking on the paths like bullets.

Our boundaries at weekends were loose. Anywhere in the village, stick with your friends and be home for tea. So it was that our gang went down to the river. How it was decided I cannot remember. There must have been seven or eight of us, I'm sure. There was a small bridge across to a wooded island. Then the river lay beyond. The bridge was a pack of ice. We leapt up and down, splintering the ice, laughing. The little island was a white world of play. The river was frozen over. There was an old wrecked boat underneath the bridge. Richard sat in it and Jenny jumped in beside him.

Jeers and cheers. Fresh snowfalls the day before gave us snowballs. Roger, the largest and strongest of us, dumped snow down my back, opening up my collar and pushing a huge snowball down my spine. I can still feel the cold and hear my scream.

But it was one of the girls, Freya her name was, who took it further.

'Let's walk right across the river!'

She just did it. Immediately. She was tiny with a small mouth and red bobble hat like a blob. In class she said nothing, just tiny giggles like bubbles; but here she moved out onto the river and there was suddenly a strange kind of quiet.

Jenny leaned out on to the edge of the boat and told her to come back.

'Not Freya Davis,' said Chris, 'I don't believe it!'

Roger hurled a snowball right out into the middle of the river but it only brushed Freya's fair, wiry hair.

'It's safe you lot,' said Richard, 'the adults have been walking on ponds and rivers for a month. We've got a television. You can see pictures of the Thames frozen.'

We were unsure. Our parents let us out to wander but what if we crossed the lines they set?

Freya stood poised in the middle. She had those giggles blowing from her mouth. Roger tried another snowball but missed. A couple of others joined in. She made herself a sitting target.

One snowball landed splat on her face and slid down her long, pointy chin. She still giggled and then positioned herself just under the bridge and it all began.

I remember it best as the snow fell, thick flakes descending across the little island, down on to our hats and scarves and across the icy river. Freya, in a kind of white haze to us, now began to dance. She began to dance on the ice without skates. She began to pirouette and she even kept her grip somehow up on her toes. Freya Davis was incredible. Freya Davis turned again and again and again on one spot, never looking like falling, never looking anything but graceful, two hands held high at times, the same faraway look on her face.

The snowball torture stopped.

Maybe it was me, maybe it was Chris, but we started to clap and, as the snow began to cover Freya, we cheered too! She moved under the bridge and through to the other side. Two adults walking a dog stopped in wonder. Was this impromptu dance on the ice something to stop or something to applaud? They just stood in a trance.

Freya twisted and turned; she once again pirouetted; she moved further downstream away from the island but we followed along the bank like disciples.

Suddenly she fell. There was a crack.

This time the two adults from the bridge stirred to action. Their golden retriever barked, pulling at his leash. But in 1963 the winter's grip was solid and thick. The crack was nothing but a hairline split. Freya's snow dance, insane at any other time, ended in triumph as she tripped back to the island's edge.

From the moment she walked back into the white wood she was quiet again. After the cheering, we were silent too. No one said much. Jenny said she was sure Freya had mentioned dancing lessons once. Freya flicked her wiry hair, dusted down her duffle coat and smoothed snow away from the toggles. She made off towards home. The others turned back for snow fights but I could not let it go somehow. I turned my small fingers around in my pocket and found a sweet.

'Freya ...'

She turned. I saw that long pointy chin and nose with the small mouth which smiled now.

'That was ... that was ... well ... here have this ...'

I handed her the sweet into a mittened hand. I had felt the shape of the sweet but not realised it was a Love Heart. She looked down. It was a red one.

'Be mine' it said.

Freya turned her mitten over the Love Heart and walked home.

The river has never frozen again like that, and the winter of 1963 went on until March. There were car rallies on the Thames and winter fairs on the pond; but I struggled to forget the wild, white dance and the mitten closing over the Love Heart like a door.

Glossary

Ambiguity

If something is ambiguous it is open to interpretation. To practise inference and deduction, your pupils need to read more texts with a level of ambiguity. This should then start to inform their own writing ideas.

Bookends

If you supply some beginnings and endings then your pupils can practise plot possibilities for the central content. This helps them to learn how to think through ideas and choose the ones with the most potential.

Chart attack

There are any number of ways in which pupils can engage with the text by comparing, contrasting, listing or questioning, using simple charts as aids.

Continuum line

Once you have set two ends of a continuum, the pupils can decide which words or ideas belong at which place along the line. Discourage rapid decision making on 'right' or 'wrong' and instead encourage reflection and the weighing of ideas using evidence. You could say to your pupils, 'To what extent do you think …?' You could first debate a position as a class and then ask the children to stand on a continuum line at the front of the classroom. Explore the issue or idea further and then see who has adjusted their position.

Core reading

An alternative phrase for **link reading**. It emphasises how vital reading is for the children.

Denouement

Most stories need some kind of resolution or climax – the denouement – when everything is explained. But writers achieve this in many different ways – often defying convention!

Didactic teaching

This phrase has been used for a long time to describe traditional teacher instruction. On those occasions when new knowledge needs to be explained or pupils guided very definitely, a didactic method can be employed with success. Outstanding teachers know how to adapt teaching styles and choose the right methodology for the right objective.

Dig deeper

This phrase has been used most in association with theories of mastery learning, where it is vital to support deeper learning on rich objectives rather than skim the surface and move on quickly.

Evidence circles

Try turning your classroom into a place where reasons always have to be found for views and opinions. Bring the reasons into an evidence circle for discussion.

Evidence spotlight

After all sorts of evidence has been collected to answer a rich, conceptual question, put the spotlight on the most convincing reasoning.

Excellent responses will (include)

This is a suggested way of ensuring that the most ambitious criteria for success are presented up front. It supports classroom discussions about how the most ambitious challenge can be achieved.

Explore and explain

This strategy can be applied to improve engagement with the text as a whole. Explaining the ideas which emerge can then become more ingrained in classroom practice.

Flow

Flow is a state of absorbed and energised concentration which was first identified by the Hungarian psychologist Mihaly Csikszentmihalyi. When we are fully immersed in an activity we are said to be in 'flow'.

Hardest question first

This represents a reversal from the traditional linear method of moving from easy to hard. It can be very revealing and surprising, but it must be accompanied by support strategies so that approaches can be personalised according to progress. It is always important to 'plan from the top' to include able learners but there are knock-on benefits for all the class. It does not mean that basic comprehension questions are not needed, but it encourages us to ask questions about when we set them and for whom.

Iambic

In poetry, an unstressed followed by a stressed beat is called an iamb.

Inform and infer

Develop the habit of sifting out the facts from the meaning between the lines. Explore clear and certain information compared with hidden meanings and suggestions. It is a very helpful access strategy which the pupils can start to apply to any unseen text.

Javelin

This is a way of visualising fast, challenging questions or tasks, aimed high and with few processes planned.

Key image strategy

Encourage the habit of identifying which images are the most significant and considering how images may link together to develop meaning for the reader.

Learning prompts

Learning through further questioning builds an enquiring classroom. Learning prompts is a phrase which could represent any kind of subtle **signposting** to deeper knowledge and which avoids giving answers too easily.

Link reading

In your lessons, try cross-referencing books and poems which you expect your pupils to read. This prevents **wider reading** from becoming an optional or a discrete part of the curriculum. Ensure link reading is mapped in as part of continuity and progression.

Listen, learn, apply

This sequence can be used whenever you want to encourage a focus on pupils listening to each other's work, so they learn about new techniques or ideas and are then ready to apply the learning in their own draft or continuation.

Metre

Metre is a unit of verse which can be used in many different combinations. See http://www.poetryarchive.org/glossary/metre for a brief guide.

Mind link

A strategy to constantly relate the themes in a text to personal experience.

Mini-plenary

These are feedback sessions with huge opportunities for learning. There should be the chance to share, question and explore progress. You can also teach explicit aspects of spelling, punctuation and grammar in context. Deeper learning and improved outcomes can then follow. Suggested questions might be: What have you found hard? What has interested you the most? How can you improve your writing? What progress have you made?

Motif

A motif is a recurring idea or theme which may be expressed figuratively or imaginatively to great effect.

Music moments

If you can find suitable music to play alongside a PowerPoint loop of slides or a reading of a text, it will do more than just add background – it will support understanding. Try getting your pupils to choose appropriate music they have found on the internet. It will be a test of how much they have internalised about the tone and emphasis of the text.

New learning

However obvious it seems, every lesson must include the opportunity for new knowledge and learning – even for the most able pupils in the class.

Noticed/noted/not sure

This is a lively thinking sequence to encourage independence, observation and questioning. Pupils have to read any kind of text – visual, media or literary – and respond in three ways:

1. Devise a list of 'noticed' puzzlements in the text.

2. Note down the most important techniques or questions.

3. Include in a third column any other questions.

There should always be words, stylistic points or unusual content which even the most able are not sure about. This will set up your explicit teaching.

Paradox

A paradox is where there seems to be a contradiction or an absurdity, but actually there may be some truth emerging from the contradiction.

Personification

This is a figure of speech which your pupils can use to breathe life and personality into something which is normally inanimate.

Philosophy for Children

See the Sapere website (http://www.sapere.org.uk) for more details on P4C and successful ways to inspire thinking and questioning.

Plus, minus, interesting

PMI is a popular **thinking engine** which can support the weighing up of observations and opinions. It's the 'interesting' column which stretches pupils the most, so why not start with that?

Prediction reversal

Instead of predicting plot developments or beginnings into endings, why not predict beginnings from endings? This gives a more challenging comprehension journey and produces very inspiring and quirky writing.

Quality options

If you ask your pupils to look at the options for quality writing, you are asking them to weigh up, in a reflective way, what title to choose. Which title can produce the most inspired work?

Question master

If you can pair up pupils to ask each other (i.e. their **talking partner**) questions on unseen texts, it can give useful practice in understanding the power of questioning.

Radial questions

Instead of setting out questions in a traditional linear way, why not offer possibilities for radiating outwards from a central, high level question? This gives you the chance to personalise support and introduce new challenges as appropriate. It is a flexible strategy and encourages the pupils to focus on the quality answers needed.

Reading journey

Instead of using the term comprehension, why not talk about reading journeys? Emphasise that active and independent approaches to reading make understanding harder texts exciting and full of enquiry – a reading journey for life!

Rhyming couplet

Two lines of verse which rhyme.

Routes to quality writing

The 'Opening Doors' strategies work on the basis that there are many different ways to teach English and many different ways in which pupils can fulfil themselves as writers and improve their basic literacy. Pupils take more responsibility for their learning by making informed choices about their planning and titles.

Signposting

All kinds of vital prompts can signpost deeper learning opportunities and create an ethos of enquiry in the classroom. Questions which simply persist in making the learner go deeper might include, 'Can you explain fully?' or 'Is there a better answer?' Socratic questioning can help here. See: http://changingminds.org/techniques/questioning/socratic_questions.htm.

Stanza

A stanza is a verse of poetry.

Talking partners

A common way of sharing but also improving ideas is to discuss drafts with a talking partner. I recommend varying talking partners throughout a term.

Taster draft

The access strategies should include an early chance to write. This kind of draft should be enriching, not laborious. Your young writers can experiment with style and get advice from you at the point of the most intense enjoyment and learning. The taster draft is a powerful learning vehicle for the improved full version they will write later on.

Text ownership

The success of the access strategies should deepen engagement and independence so that the pupil 'owns' the text rather than the teacher. Ideas can then be borrowed from the text for quality writing.

Think, pair, share

A popular **thinking engine** where all pupils reflect in silence on a challenging question, then share their thoughts with a **talking partner**. In this way, participation can be expected from all in a whole-class debate.

Thinking engine

A generic phrase used to sum up the many ways in which the level of thinking can be developed in a classroom. However, the starting point is having something challenging and interesting to apply the thinking to!

White space thinking

This is a very common but effective strategy for encouraging pupils to write notes and questions in the spaces around texts, rather than being limited to answers in boxes.

Wider reading

The traditional phrase for reading on the periphery of your subject. I advise using the term **link reading** in order to raise expectations and support cross-referencing in lessons.

Wings to fly

The phrase, 'Wings to fly, not drills to kill', comes from a wonderful course evaluation by a teacher about how her pupils could benefit from more open and creative approaches. Risk-taking lies at the heart of any possibility for pupils to fly. They will do what we expect, so we should signify that writing in unusual ways is exciting. Of course, some will still need formats and templates as support resources.

Zooming in

Using the language of media studies can be very useful. Just as a camera zooms in, so too can a teacher offer a magnified view of a particular image or concept by focusing on one part of the text. A visualiser can provide a quite literal 'zoom in' on the subject.

Bibliography

Primary sources

Andersen, Hans Christian (2014 [1836]). *The Little Mermaid*, tr. Henry H. B. Paull, ill. Vilhelm Pedersen and Helen Stratton. N.p.: Hythloday Press.

Arnold, Matthew (2015 [1849]). 'The Forsaken Merman', in *The Strayed Reveller and Other Poems* (Classic Reprint Series). Kila, MT: Kessinger Publishing.

Auden, W. H. (2012 [1936]). 'The Night Mail', in Allie Esiri and Rachel Kelly (eds), *A Treasury of Poems for Almost Every Possibility*. Edinburgh: Canongate Books.

Baldwin, James (1968). *Grandad with Snails*. London: Hutchinson Educational.

Barrett Browning, Elizabeth (2015 [1850]). 'How Do I Love Thee', in Dr Sally Minogue (ed.), *The Collected Poems of Elizabeth Barrett Browning*. London: Wordsworth Editions.

Baum, L. Frank (2007 [1900]). *The Wonderful Wizard of Oz*. London: Penguin.

Blackman, Malorie (2006). *Noughts and Crosses*. London: Corgi.

Bloom, Valerie (2001). 'Total Solar Eclipse', in *The World is Sweet*. London: Bloomsbury.

Brontë, Charlotte (1997 [1848]). 'Mementos', in *The Brontës*. London: Everyman's Poetry.

Brontë, Charlotte (2006 [1847]). *Jane Eyre*. London: Penguin.

Brontë, Emily (1995 [1847]). *Wuthering Heights*. Oxford: Oxford World's Classics.

Buchan, John (1993 [1915]). *The Thirty-Nine Steps*. Ware: Wordsworth Editions.

Burnford, Sheila (2004 [1960]). *The Incredible Journey*. London: Penguin.

Carroll, Lewis (2007 [1871]). *Through the Looking Glass*. London: Penguin.

Clare, John (1992(1835]). 'The Mouse's Nest', in *The Essential Clare*. New York: Ecco Press.

Collins, Wilkie (1974 [1868]). *The Woman in White*. Harmondsworth: Penguin.

Collins, Wilkie (1993 [1869]). *The Moonstone*. Ware: Wordsworth Editions.

Conan Doyle, Arthur (1992 [1892]). *The Adventures of Sherlock Holmes*. Ware: Wordsworth Editions.

Conan Doyle, Arthur (1995 [1912]). *The Lost World*. Ware: Wordsworth Editions.

Conan Doyle, Arthur (1999 [1901]). 'The Hound of the Baskervilles', in *The Hound of the Baskervilles and The Valley of Fear.* Ware: Wordsworth Editions.

Crichton, Michael (1990). *Jurassic Park.* London: Arrow.

Dahl, Roald (2013 [1984]). *Boy: Tales of Childhood.* London: Puffin.

Davis, A. R. (ed.) (1971). *The Penguin Book of Chinese Verse,* tr. Robert Kotewall and Norman L. Smith. London: Penguin.

de la Mare, Walter (1941). 'The Magnifying Glass', in *Bells and Grass: A Book of Rhymes.* London: Faber and Faber.

de la Mare, Walter (1979 [1912]). 'All That's Past', in *Walter de la Mare: Collected Poems.* London: Faber and Faber.

de la Mare, Walter (1979 [1912]). 'Arabia', in *Walter de la Mare: Collected Poems.* London: Faber and Faber.

de la Mare, Walter (1979 [1912]). 'The Listeners', in *Walter de la Mare: Collected Poems.* London: Faber and Faber.

de la Mare, Walter (1979 [1933]). 'A Robin', in *Walter de la Mare: Collected Poems.* London: Faber and Faber.

de la Mare, Walter (1989 [1920]). 'Nicholas Nye', in *Collected Rhymes and Verses.* London: Faber and Faber.

de la Mare, Walter (1989 [1920]). 'Silver', in *Collected Rhymes and Verses.* London: Faber and Faber.

Dickens, Charles (1994 [1861]). *Great Expectations.* London: Penguin Popular Classics.

Dickens, Charles (2003 [1837]). *Oliver Twist.* London: Penguin.

Dickens, Charles (2003 [1852]). *Bleak House.* London: Penguin.

Dickinson, Emily (2002 [1886]). 'Snake', in *Collected Poems of Emily Dickinson.* New York: Gramercy.

Dickinson, Emily (2002 [1891]). 'A Thunderstorm', in *Collected Poems of Emily Dickinson.* New York: Gramercy.

Dickinson, Emily (2002 [1891]). 'Hope', in *Collected Poems of Emily Dickinson.* New York: Gramercy.

Dickinson, Emily (2002 [1896]). 'The Sea of Sunset', in *Collected Poems of Emily Dickinson.* New York: Gramercy.

Dickinson, Emily (2014 [1891]). 'I Started Early – Took my Dog', in *Poetry Please.* London: Faber and Faber.

Edwards, Amelia B. (2010 [1864]). 'The Phantom Coach', in Vic Parker (ed.), *Classic Ghost Stories.* Thaxted: Miles Kelly.

Eliot, George (1996 [1876]). *Daniel Deronda.* Ware: Wordsworth Editions.

Farjeon, Eleanor (1979). 'It Was Long Ago', in Kaye Webb (ed.), *I Like This Poem.* Harmondsworth: Puffin.

Gaiman, Neil (2009). *The Graveyard Book.* London: Bloomsbury.

Gaiman, Neil (2013). *Coraline.* London: Bloomsbury.

Gaiman, Neil (2014). *The Sleeper and the Spindle.* London: Bloomsbury.

Garner, Alan (2014). *The Owl Service.* London: HarperCollins Children's Books.

Hardy, Thomas (1957 [1892]). *Tess of the D'Urbervilles.* London: Macmillan.

Hardy, Thomas (1974 [1917]). 'Heredity', in *The Complete Poems of Thomas Hardy.* London: Macmillan.

Hardy, Thomas (1974 [1919]). 'Old Furniture', in T. R. M. Creighton (ed.), *Poems of Thomas Hardy*. London: Macmillan.

Hardy, Thomas (1974 [1919]). 'The Clock-Winder', in T. R. M. Creighton (ed.), *Poems of Thomas Hardy*. London: Macmillan.

Hardy, Thomas (1974 [1919]). 'The Haunter', in T. R. M. Creighton (ed.), *Poems of Thomas Hardy*. London: Macmillan.

Hardy, Thomas (1974 [1919]). 'The Little Old Table', in T. R. M. Creighton (ed.), *Poems of Thomas Hardy*. London: Macmillan.

Hardy, Thomas (1974 [1919]). 'The Musical Box', in T. R. M. Creighton (ed.), *Poems of Thomas Hardy*. London: Macmillan.

Hardy, Thomas (1974 [1919]). 'The Photograph', in T. R. M. Creighton (ed.), *Poems of Thomas Hardy*. London: Macmillan.

Hardy, Thomas (1974 [1919]). 'To My Father's Violin', in T. R. M. Creighton (ed.), *Poems of Thomas Hardy*. London: Macmillan.

Hardy, Thomas (1974 [1919]). 'Voices from Things Growing in a Churchyard', in T. R. M. Creighton (ed.), *Poems of Thomas Hardy*). London: Macmillan.

Hardy, Thomas (1974 [1919]). 'Where the Picnic Was', in T. R. M. Creighton (ed.), *Poems of Thomas Hardy*. London: Macmillan.

Hardy, Thomas (1993 [1874]). *Far From the Madding Crowd*. London: Macmillan.

Hardy, Thomas (1995 [1888]). *Wessex Tales*. Ware: Wordsworth Editions.

Hemingway, Ernest (2000 [1951]). *The Old Man and the Sea*. London: Vintage.

Hilton, James (2015 [1933]). *Lost Horizon*. London: Vintage.

Hodgson Burnett, Frances (2007 [1911]). *The Secret Garden*. Oxford: Oxford Children's Classics.

Hood, Thomas (2013 [1826]). 'I Remember, I Remember', in Roger McGough (ed.), *Poetry Please*. London: Faber and Faber.

Household, Geoffrey (2002 [1939]). *Rogue Male*. London: Orion.

Housman, A. E. (1994 [1896]). 'Blue Remembered Hills', in *The Collected Poems of A. E. Housman*. Ware: Wordsworth Editions.

Hughes, Ted (2005 [1970]). 'Amulet' in *Collected Poems for Children*. London: Faber and Faber.

Hughes, Ted (2005). *Collected Poems for Children*. London: Faber and Faber.

Irving, Washington (1968 [1819]). 'Rip Van Winkle', in *The Legend of Sleepy Hollow and Other Stories*. London: Minster Classics.

Irving, Washington (2000 [1820]). *The Legend of Sleepy Hollow*. London: Penguin.

Kafka, Franz (2014 [1915]). *Metamorphosis*, in *The Essential Kafka*. Ware: Wordsworth Classics.

Kafka, Franz (2014 [1922]). *The Castle*, in *The Essential Kafka*. Ware: Wordsworth Editions.

Kästner, Erich (2012 [1931]). *Emil and the Detectives*. London: Vintage.

Kipling, Rudyard (2012 [1910]). 'If', in Allie Esiri and Rachel Kelly (eds), *A Treasury of Poems for Almost Every Possibility.* Edinburgh: Canongate Books.

Lee, Laurie (2014 [1959]). *Cider with Rosie.* London: Vintage.

London, Jack (1977 [1908]). *That Spot*, in *Short Stories One.* Huddersfield: Schofield & Sims.

London, Jack (1992 [1903 and 1906]). *Call of the Wild and White Fang.* Ware: Wordsworth Editions.

London, Jack (2008 [1908]). *To Build a Fire and Other Favorite Stories.* Mineola, NY: Dover Thrift Editions.

Longfellow, Henry Wadsworth (1994 [1855]). *The Song of Hiawatha*, in *The Works of Henry Wadsworth Longfellow.* Ware: Wordsworth Editions.

Longfellow, Henry Wadsworth (1994 [1858]). 'Haunted Houses', in *The Works of Henry Wadsworth Longfellow.* Ware: Wordsworth Editions.

Longfellow, Henry Wadsworth (1994 [1880]). 'The Tide Rises, the Tide Falls', in *The Works of Henry Wadsworth Longfellow.* Ware: Wordsworth Editions.

Marks, Leo (1999 [1943]). 'Code Poem for the French Resistance', in *The Life That I Have.* London: Souvenir Press.

Marlowe, Christopher (2003 [1604]). *Dr Faustus*, Roma Gill (ed.). London: Methuen.

Masefield, John (2010 [1917]). 'Unending Sky', in *Lollingdown Downs and Other Poems.* Whitefish, MT: Kessinger Publishing.

Masefield, John (2012 [1916]). 'Sea Fever', in *Salt Water Poems and Ballads.* London: Forgotten Books.

Morpurgo, Michael (2008). *Born to Run.* London: HarperCollins.

Morpurgo, Michael (2011). *Why the Whales Came.* London: Egmont.

Nicholson, William (2000). *The Wind Singer.* London: Egmont.

Nicholson, William (2001). *Slaves of the Mastery.* London: Egmont.

Nicholson, William (2002). *Firesong.* London: Egmont.

Owen, Wilfred (1994 [1913]). 'The Unreturning', in *The War Poems of Wilfred Owen.* London: Chatto and Windus.

Plath, Sylvia (2002 [1960]). 'Mirror', in *Collected Poems.* London: Faber and Faber.

Plath, Sylvia (2002). *The Unabridged Journals of Sylvia Plath.* New York: First Anchor.

Poe, Edgar Allan (1989 [1844]). 'A Tale of the Ragged Mountains', in *Ten Great Mysteries.* New York: Scholastic.

Poe, Edgar Allan (1993 [1841]). 'A Descent into the Maelstrom', in *Tales of Mystery and Imagination.* Ware: Wordsworth Editions.

Poe, Edgar Allan (1993 [1843]). 'The Tell-Tale Heart', in *Tales of Mystery and Imagination.* Ware: Wordsworth Editions.

Poe, Edgar Allan (2012 [1841]). *The Murders in the Rue Morgue and Other Tales.* London: Penguin.

Reeves, James (2009 [1950]). 'A Mermaid Song', in *Complete Poems for Children.* London: Faber and Faber.

Reeves, James (2009 [1950]). 'The Sea', in *Complete Poems for Children*. London: Faber and Faber.

Reeves, James (2009 [1952]). 'A Garden at Night', in *Complete Poems for Children*. London: Faber and Faber.

Serraillier, Ian (2012 [1956]). *The Silver Sword*. London: Vintage.

Shakespeare, William (2015[1593]). *Shakespeare's Sonnets*. London: Penguin Classics.

Shelley, Percy Bysshe (2002 [1818]). 'Ozymandias', in *The Selected Poetry and Prose of Shelley*. Ware: Wordsworth Poetry Library.

Shelley, Mary (1992 [1818]). *Frankenstein*. Ware: Wordsworth Editions.

Smith, Dodie (2002 [1956]). *The Hundred and One Dalmatians*. London: Penguin.

Smith, Dodie (2004 [1948]). *I Capture the Castle*. London: Vintage.

Steinbeck, John (2011 [1937]). *The Red Pony*. London: Puffin.

Steinbeck, John (2011 [1947]). *The Pearl*. London: Puffin.

Stevenson, Robert Louis (1993 [1886]). *The Strange Case of Dr Jekyll and Mr Hyde*. Ware: Wordsworth Editions.

Stoker, Bram (2004 [1897]). *Dracula*. London: Penguin.

Strong, Jeremy (2007). *The Hundred-Mile-An-Hour Dog*. London: Puffin.

Taylor, G. P. (2003). *Shadowmancer*. London: Faber and Faber.

Tennyson, Alfred Lord (1994 [1830]). 'The Mermaid', in *The Works of Alfred Lord Tennyson*, Ware: Wordsworth Editions.

Tennyson, Alfred Lord (1994 [1859]). 'The Kraken', in *The Works of Alfred Lord Tennyson*. Ware: Wordsworth Editions.

Thomas, Dylan (1983 [1940]). 'A Visit to Grandpa's', in *Collected Stories*. London: Dent.

Tolkien, J. R. R. (2007 [1954–1955]). *The Lord of the Rings*. London: HarperCollins.

Verne, Jules (1996 [1864]). *Journey to the Centre of the Earth*. Ware: Wordsworth Editions.

Wells, H. G. (2005 [1895]). *The Time Machine*. London: Penguin.

Wells, H. G. (2005 [1896]). *The Island of Dr Moreau*. London: Penguin.

Wells, H. G. (2005 [1901]). *The First Men in the Moon*. London: Penguin.

Wells, H. G. (2012 [1897]). *The Invisible Man*. London: Penguin.

Wilde, Oscar (1992 [1890]). *The Picture of Dorian Gray*. Ware: Wordsworth Editions.

Yeats, W. B. (2000 [1919]). 'An Irish Airman Foresees His Death', in *The Collected Poems of W. B. Yeats*. Ware: Wordsworth Editions.

Zephaniah, Benjamin (1999). *Face*. London: Bloomsbury.

Secondary sources

Alexander, Robin (2008). *Towards Dialogic Teaching: Rethinking Classroom Talk*, 4th edn. Cambridge: Dialogos.

Clymer, Theodore (1968). 'What is "Reading"? Some Current Concepts', in Helen M. Robinson (ed.), *Innovation and Change in Reading Instruction*. Sixty-Seventh Yearbook of the National Society for the Study of Education. Chicago, IL: University of Chicago Press, pp. 17–23.

Biggs, J. and Collis, K. (1982). *Evaluating the Quality of Learning: SOLO Taxonomy*. New York: Academic Press.

Bowen, John and Dinsdale, Ann (n.d.). 'The Brontës' Early Writings: Combining Fantasy and Fact', *British Library*. Available at: http://www.bl.uk/ romantics-and-victorians/videos/ brontes-early-writings.

Claxton, Guy (2002). *Building Learning Power*. Bristol: TLO Ltd.

Dean, Geoff (2008). *English for Gifted and Talented Students: 11–18 Years*. London: Sage.

English, David (1998). *Slipping the Surly Bonds: Great Quotations on Flight*. New York: McGraw-Hill.

Eyre, Deborah (2016). 'Beyond Gifted', *National Education Trust* (12 February). Available at: http://www. nationaleducationtrust.net/ ShapingIdeasShapingLives238.php.

Forster, E. M. (2005 [1927]). *Aspects of the Novel*. London: Penguin.

Goodwin, Prue (ed.) (2004). *Literacy Through Creativity*. London: David Fulton.

Haas, Ray (2014). *Touching the Face of God: The Story of John Gillespie Magee, Jr. and His Poem 'High Flight'*. Wilson, NC: High Flight Productions.

Hughes, Ted (2008 [1967]). *Poetry in the Making: A Handbook for Writing and Teaching*. London: Faber & Faber.

McGough, Roger (2015). 'Between the Lines', *Teach Reading and Writing* (August): 81.

Miller, Donalyn (2009). *The Book Whisperer: Awakening the Inner Reader in Every Child*. San Francisco, CA: Jossey-Bass.

Moses, Brian (n.d.). Children's Literature Interest Group: Interview with Brian Moses [by Brenda Marshall and Nicky Potter], *English Association*. Available at; http://www2.le.ac.uk/offices/ english-association/sigs/ childrens-literature/authors/brian-moses.

Myhill, Debra (2015). 'Words with Ways: How Grammar Supports Writing'. Available at: https://www.researchgate. net/publication/265743541_Words_with_ Ways_How_Grammar_supports_Writing.

Rowling, J. K. (2008). *Very Good Lives: The Fringe Benefits of Failure and the Importance of Imagination*. London: Sphere.

West-Burnham, John and Coates, Max (2005). *Personalizing Learning: Transforming Education for Every Child*. Stafford: Network Educational Press.

Useful websites

Malorie Blackman www.malorieblackman.
co.uk
Book Trust www.booktrust.org.uk
Centre for Literacy in Primary Education
www.clpe.org.uk
Children's Laureate www.
childrenslaureate.org.uk
English and Media Centre www.
englishandmedia.co.uk
English Association: 4–11 online articles
www2.le.ac.uk/offices/
english-association/primary/
primary-plus/411online
Film Education www.filmclub.org
Literacy Shed www.literacyshed.com
London Gifted and Talented www.
londongt.org
More Able and Talented (Wales) http://
matwales.org
National Association for the Teaching of
English www.nate.org.uk
National Literacy Trust www.literacytrust.
org.uk
National Poetry Day www.
nationalpoetryday.co.uk
Playing by the Book www.
playingbythebook.net
Poetry Archive www.poetryarchive.org
Poetry by Heart www.poetrybyheart.org.uk
Poetry Society www.poetrysociety.org.uk
Potential Plus UK www.potentialplusuk.
org
Michael Rosen www.michaelrosen.co.uk

Society for the Advancement of
Philosophical Enquiry and Reflection in
Education www.sapere.org.uk
Socratic questions http://changingminds.
org/techniques/questioning/socratic_
questions.htm
SOLO Taxonomy www.
learningandteaching.info/learning/solo.
htm
United Kingdom Literacy Association
https://ukla.org